Heart
of the Matter

How to Find Love,
How to Make It Work

Linda Austin, M.D.

ATRIA BOOKS

New York   London   Toronto   Sydney   Singapore

ATRIA BOOKS
1230 Avenue of the Americas
New York, NY 10020

ISBN: 0-7434-3771-3

First Atria Books hardcover printing May 2003

10   9   8   7   6   5   4   3   2   1

ATRIA BOOKS is a trademark of Simon & Schuster, Inc.

Manufactured in the United States of America

For information regarding special discounts for bulk purchases,
please contact Simon & Schuster Special Sales at 1-800-456-6798
or business@simonandschuster.com

Heart
of the Matter

Also by Linda Austin, M.D.

What's Holding You Back?: Eight Critical Choices for Women's Success

To my beloved husband, Jeb

ACKNOWLEDGMENTS

This book was conceived one evening in New York City over dinner with my literary agent, Barbara Lowenstein. Barbara has an extraordinary ability to discern what "works" from what doesn't, and an unflinching commitment to guide her authors to their best effort. She helped develop and refine the original blueprint of the book, and I appreciate her enormous contribution.

My husband, Jeb Hallett, was the inspiration for many of the ideas in the book. We spent long hours discussing basic concepts, sometimes during walks and drives in the New England countryside, sometimes by the fire in our living room, and often in early morning conversations when we awakened, for morning is my best time for thinking. The chapter on Engagement was completely inspired by watching Jeb in action, for he is the most deeply engaged person I know.

My editor at Atria Books is Brenda Copeland, and I thank Brenda from the bottom of my heart for all the help she gave me. Brenda has the unique ability to offer criticism laced with so much humor, praise, and encouragement that I loved our conversations even when they resulted in giving the heave-ho to large, cherished chunks of material. As this project developed, I increasingly wrote this book to Brenda and for Brenda. Coach, teacher, critic, friend: thanks for being a true partner in this project, Brenda.

Some of the ideas in this book were original, while many were drawn from some of the great psychoanalytic thinkers of the twentieth century. There are three major lines of psychoanalytic thinking: ego psychology, self psychology, and object relations theory, and I have used the best ideas of all, leaning heavily on the contributions of writers like Sigmund and Anna Freud, Klein, Fairbairn, Winnicott, Kohut, Masterson, and Kernberg in the concepts of this book. In my own development as a psychiatrist, I owe a debt of gratitude to my many supervisors and teachers, chief among them Larry Inderbitzin.

Finally, I want to thank the people who have loved me the longest: my parents, Robert and Elpidia Smith, who offered me the unconditional love that every child needs. They were extraordinarily disciplined, committed parents, and I appreciate all they have done for me. I can only thank them by passing their gift of love on to my own children, Matt and Stephanie, my greatest sources of joy and hope for the future.

CONTENTS

INTRODUCTION

You know what it feels like when "something's missing."

You sense a vague discomfort, a whiff of uneasy numbness that creeps up during quiet moments. *Nonsense,* you scold yourself. *Snap out of it. There's no reason to mope. Don't let anyone notice. I have so much to be grateful for.*

A few hours, a few days, pass. *There it is again. That flatness. I feel like I'm just going through the motions. I hope no one notices.*

Perhaps that feeling steals over you when you least expect it, at times when you really ought to feel happy. You may be in a decent relationship and can't quite figure out what's wrong. Where's that sense of detachment coming from? Is there something wrong with your relationship? Or is something wrong within you?

Maybe it's clear to you that there *is* something wrong with your current relationship. You just don't feel an exchange with your "other." No connection. Perhaps your interactions feel hollow, maybe even contentious, and you're not sure what to do about it. Whose fault is it? Can you fix it, or is this what happens to all long-term relationships?

Or perhaps you know there's something missing because you're not in a love relationship at all. Maybe it's been so long since you've dated that when your friend asked you if you were seeing someone, you thought she meant a psychiatrist. You've learned to keep a stiff upper lip. You have good friends and you like your job.

But all too frequently you have that thought: *There's something missing*.

And you know what it is: love.

Love is a vital emotional nutrient. In its absence you experience psychological hunger pains, a gnawing sense of inner emptiness. In small doses, lack of love produces brief pangs that send you scurrying to connect with someone, like a dieter who can't pass by the refrigerator without making a raid. But just as prolonged physical starvation actually becomes painful, prolonged lack of love inflicts an emotional pain of its own.

Whether your starvation is caused by an unsatisfying relationship or by having no relationship at all, you have just two ways to respond to the "something's missing" feeling. The first is to "try harder" to connect with others. If you're in a relationship, you "try harder" with your "other." You get a new outfit, suggest a weekend away, or propose a new activity to share. You ask your mate what's wrong, and you may or may not get a reply that helps you reconnect. If you're single, you "try harder" by reaching outside your routine life. You call your friends and ask them to set you up. You scan the singles' ads on-line and in the newspaper or maybe you call a dating service. You decide to go to the next reception you're invited to—who knows, maybe there will be someone interesting there.

But if despite your best efforts you just can't reconnect with someone, you take the second choice. You begin to give up—not all at once, but in bits and pieces. You retreat from your discomfort by hiding out within your "secret self." You withdraw from your mate, zoning out in your private thoughts and fantasies. If you're single, you develop solitary routines that comfort you—pizza and a video on a Friday night, lengthy long-distance calls to friends on weekends—that ward off loneliness and fortify you as a self-contained unit. Within your secret self you create distractions that block awareness of your loneliness. You find ways to protect yourself from intimate contact with others who are disappointing or frustrating.

Hiding away in your secret self may take many forms. Maybe you escape from your current relationship by developing a big, whopping crush on someone who's out of reach; even while you're making love to your mate, you're imagining you're in the arms of another. Perhaps you spend hours slouched in front of the television, preferring to watch the battles of *Survivor* rather than fight for survival in your own family. Maybe you retreat from opportunities to meet a new love by staying in your apartment night after night, cocooned in a world of the Internet or videos. Maybe you marry your career or your aging mother or the gym down the street. Or you bury yourself in work conflicts . . . or spend hours surfing the Net . . . or become preoccupied by the ups and downs of your stock portfolio.

As you pull your heart and mind away from the reality of the here and now, you substitute a fantasy world you create for yourself. The ability to live within a world of fantasy begins at an early age, for even tiny children love the world of "Pretend." Think back to your own childhood. You may remember times when you dealt with pain, confusion, or betrayal by immersing yourself in an imaginary experience that lifted you out of the hurt of the moment.

Carrie, a woman who suffered from lifelong depression, told me how she dealt with the neglect she'd experienced in childhood from her emotionally disturbed mother. "At night, in bed, I would snuggle down in my pillow and I'd imagine that the Good Fairy was there to take care of me. The Good Fairy was my wonderful friend, like a mother and father put together for me. She was always there, making me feel loved and cared about.

"Then, as I got older, it was the Virgin Mary who was my

mother. We were raised Catholic, and the Virgin Mary was really a big thing for me. So whenever my mother failed me, which was all the time, I would just pray to the Virgin Mary and be comforted.

"My life now should be fine. I have a good job and friends who care about me. So I don't know quite why I'm depressed, except that I think that all of those years as a child have left their mark. I lived in my fantasies, but it's just not the same as having a real mother."

It's just not the same. Whether you're five or sixty-five, love in your own head is just not the same as love in the here-and-now world. As with a plant whose roots begin to shrivel and die from prolonged drought, retreating into your own head makes you progressively less able to receive emotional nutrients from the world. Your growth becomes stunted, your color fades, your spirit droops.

As disconnection progresses, a vicious cycle begins. The more you retreat, the more comfortable you become in your own world, and the harder it is to take a risk in the interpersonal world—the *real* world. As you pull away from others, they start to pull away from you as well, and your opportunities for connection diminish. What you need is a jump-start out of that vicious cycle. A concrete plan of action to get you reconnected with the human world . . . and opportunities to find love.

So What's at the Heart of the Matter?

If you are aware that your life is suffering from a love deficit, you've doubtless asked yourself the questions *Is there something wrong with me? What am I doing wrong?* You look around and see friends—or worse yet, people you can't stand—who are not as attractive or bright or even pleasant as you. Yet some of them seem to have found love, good love. If they can do it, why not you? *What's at the heart of the matter?*

In my first book, *What's Holding You Back? Eight Critical Choices for Women's Success*, I explored the "psychological glass ceiling," the emotional barriers that keep women from achieving career success. This book is about a different kind of inner glass ceiling: the one that holds you back from the heights of great love. Just as many women perceive barriers to career success as external rather than self-imposed, it's easy to believe that what holds you back from love is "out there." *There just aren't any good men out there. My work is too demanding. My first priority is raising my kids. It's hard to find someone who shares my values.*

There may well be at least a kernel of reality in all of those barriers to love. Of course it may take time to find someone who is really the right fit for you. But you may also be using those external issues as shields against looking at your internal issues. Your goal is to find ways around those problems, not to use them as barricades against love.

Why is it that love seems to come easily to some people and not to others? I'm convinced that there's nothing fundamentally wrong with those who have difficulty finding and keeping love. But there may be specific behaviors that you engage in—and specific behaviors that you do not engage in—that have a profound impact on whether you find and keep love. And I'm convinced that those behaviors can be learned, practiced, and eventually incorporated into your basic personality.

This book is based on the conviction that each of us has the ability to improve our ability to find and inspire love through specific behaviors. There are five core behaviors, Essential Practices, that will deepen and transform your ability to give and receive love and loyalty:

Engagement is the fundamental currency of love. Engagement is the way you first connect to the people you meet, and the way you remain connected with a few precious people throughout your life. There are in fact simple *terms of engagement* that you can begin to practice today that will enrich your relationship life and that will help you connect and grow in a living, breathing, dynamic exchange.

Evaluation is the process by which you thoughtfully, proactively determine who in your life is worthy of your deepest love—and of whom you are worthy. Evaluation is a rational process in which you ask the tough questions about whether a prospective relationship will really bring you happiness. It slows down the impulsiveness of your primitive brain at moments when you want to connect with someone, *anyone*, who seems to protect you from the dread of aloneness. Evaluation is essential for screening out potentially disastrous relationships, for it checks your unconscious belief that the devil you know is better than no one at all. The instinct to create powerful bonds of loyalty to others is a basic human drive that is so necessary for emotional health and well-being. Learning to channel this wonderful gift of yours, your loyalty drive, to one who is able to truly reciprocate is an Essential Practice.

Expanding your capacity to love is the third great Essential. Instinctively you recognize the danger of aloneness, with its attendant emotional starvation. But because of the power of the loyalty drive, you also fear the danger of connection, with its possibilities of suffocation and loss of freedom and control. Between those dual dangers lies your safety zone in which you feel safe and free to experiment in intimacy. The more you can expand this zone, the more comfortable you will feel when you're in an intimate relationship—and when you're experiencing important growth periods of singlehood.

The optimal psychological state for connection is one of *emo-*

tional independence, the fourth Essential. The closer a relationship is, the greater its power to trigger ancient roles and feelings that distort your ability to perceive yourself and your "other" accurately and to interact in a mature and loving way. Emotional independence is a way of understanding and actualizing the authentic "you" and to allow your "other" to maintain his or her own authenticity as well.

The fifth Essential reflects that we live long lives, growing, changing, and developing from cradle to grave. The capacity for emotional *evolution* allows you to guide your personal growth in the service of improving your relationships, and to use your relationships to stimulate your own development. At any point in which your human environment changes, you have three choices. You may choose *evolution*, gradually adapting yourself to the needs of your relationship. Alternatively, you may choose a special form of evolution, *revolution*, choosing to change your environment rather than change yourself; breaking up with your lover or spouse is an example of revolution. The third choice, *stagnation*, is an attempt not to change at all despite the changes of the world outside you. Your goal should be to make proactive choices about how you evolve, or at times, choose to revolt, and to become aware of the areas in your life in which you have become stagnant.

Erosives

As in physics, every action in emotional life potentially has an equal and opposite reaction. Just as there are behaviors that foster love, there are behaviors that kill it, and no book about helping you move toward love could be complete without exploring the ways you unwittingly damage the love that comes your way.

It's relatively easy to be aware of the big, hairy, disastrous things you can do to kill love. I call those really obvious behaviors catastrophics—things such as cheating, lying, or betraying confidences—which destroy love as predictably as a heat-seeking missiles delivering dirty bombs.

You know these things already, so there's no point in elaborating them. What is far more interesting to explore are what I call little-*e* erosives—the tiny, unconscious behaviors you engage in that imperceptibly shape your relationship, like rainwater dripping on limestone, drop by drop shaping the form of your interactions. Erosives may weaken your relationship so gradually that you may be quite unaware of the danger of an imminent collapse. Indeed, sometimes the most seemingly loyal relationships can be severely damaged by erosion, for both parties may take the love of the other so for granted that they cease to pay attention to the subtle nuances of the relationship dynamics. So as we explore the Essentials, I'll also encourage you to think about the erosives, which need to be cleaned up along the way.

Change

This book reflects twenty-five years of my life as a psychiatrist working with all sorts of people—men, women, elderly folks, teenagers, housewives, executives, homeless people—who were trying to break out of their secret selves to live more fully in the real world of loving human relationships. Several observations have been common to all:

1. Four major problems drive people to therapy: how to love, how to work, how to be happy, and how to find meaning in life. Underlying all four, however, is a core question: *How can I connect more richly to the human world around me?*

2. The default mode of the human mind is to ascribe blame to others, not to ourselves. Most people begin self-examination by first blaming others, especially parents and spouses, for their interpersonal problems and only gradually perceive their own issues. It takes great courage, humility, and self-honesty to dig within to understand why you construct your relationship world as you do.

3. The only people who do find the love and the life they want eventually give up believing they can change others and take responsibility to change themselves.

4. People who choose not to change continue to struggle with the same issues year after year . . . and sometimes decade after decade.

Zen Buddhists say that all of life is change, and all suffering comes from resisting change. Inner change is hardest of all, for it starts with the humbling realization that you have created the life you are living, and only you have the power and the responsibility to get the life you want. Indeed, life scatters a handful of seeds for you at the moment of conception, seeds that give rise to your family, your community, and the culture in which you live. But how you live within that garden, and how you decide which new plantings to bring into your life, are up to you.

The good news is, though, that making small changes in your outlook and behavior can have enormous impact on your ability to get to the heart of the matter and live the life you want. Making changes in small aspects of your human interactions—how you engage with others, how you choose your closest relationships, and how you manage your interpersonal anxiety—can have huge ripple effects on what happens to you in life. Major parts of your personality—your values, your likes and dislikes, your intelligence, your sense of humor, your life goals—may stay intact. But you'll be much more able to use those strengths to move toward the life and love you want so much.

Heart
of the Matter

CHAPTER ONE

So Just What Is Love, Anyway?

LOVE IS AN EXTRAORDINARY WORD, an infinite container for all the wishes, fantasies, needs, and impulses we have for connection. It's a one-size-fits-all term that is applied to an enormous range of relationships and emotions. Charlie Brown said that love is a warm puppy. But *love* also describes the way you feel about your mate on your wedding day; it's the way you feel about a beloved relative who is being laid to rest; and it's even the desperate wish a child has to earn the affection of an abusive parent. We call it love when you surrender to sexual union with your beloved, but it's also love that lashes you with pain when that same lover has betrayed you. Love may be as exhilarating as your wildest infatuation, as depressing as changing your demented mother's diaper, or as enraging as picking up your drunk sister at a local bar.

So what is love, anyway?

Loyalty

The basic instinct uniting all of these experiences has nothing whatever to do with the feel-good quality we commonly think of as love. *Rather, the core of love is loyalty, simple, blind loyalty.* In *Porgy and Bess*, Bess described it well:

> *Maybe he's lazy, maybe he's slow*
> *Maybe I'm crazy, baby I know*
> *Can't help lovin' that man of mine.*

"Can't help lovin' " is the strongest bond of connection a human can feel. That recognition of core loyalty as the basis for love appears over and over again in human culture. Our wedding vows promise love "for better or worse." Our marines pledge *Semper fidelis*. Even children cement their loyalty to their friends by pricking their skin and becoming blood brothers or sisters.

Go a bit deeper, though, and it's obvious that the drive to be loyal isn't even uniquely human at all. It's embedded within animal nature and may be particularly strong within some mammalian species. Primates live in troops and establish relationships of loyalty and obedience to other individual animals. Dogs are remarkably loyal, even reaching outside their own species to form lifelong relationships; God give us the strength to be the people our dogs think we are. Tiny mountain voles form bonded relationships, living as lifelong monogamous pairs in furry affection. It's clear that the drive to be loyal to *specific, familiar individuals* is hardwired in evolutionarily ancient centers of our brains. The power of the drive emerges in human infancy, for by seven months babies howl in protest if they are held by a stranger. Love is an instinct that's central to our human, even our animal, nature, and you shouldn't try to fool Mother Nature.

Given the power of loyalty, if you could learn to really harness and direct that drive, your life would be graced with an enhanced sense of meaning and fulfillment. If you were able to inspire the loyalty of those you care about—inspire and maintain it throughout your lifetime—imagine how enriched every aspect of your life would feel. If you were able to channel your own ability to remain loyal—to choose the right people to love, to nurture and sustain that love throughout your life—imagine how sustaining your relationships would feel.

Hidden Dangers of Loyalty

But as powerful and wonderful as loyalty is, it does carry hidden dangers.

The first danger is that in a long-term committed relationship it's easy to take your "other's" loyalty for granted. You may become so convinced that it's an entitlement you've earned through the passage of time or shared hardship that you become insensitive to strains you are placing on the relationship. Loyalty is indeed powerful, but it's not absolutely reliable. Two people in a relationship may have very different levels of loyalty, and very different tolerance for the stresses that erode love. The increasing rates of divorce and infidelity in our society are testimony that loyalty can be overridden by many factors. When that happens, the spouse who has been faithful often feels blindsided. In fact it may be that their loyalty itself was a blindfold, blocking their view of problems.

The second danger is that you *both* may take loyalty so for granted that you've stopped asking important questions about your relationship. You're not in danger of losing the relationship, but questions like "Are we happy?" or "Are we really good for each other?" aren't addressed. For some couples, their loyalty carries a self-righteous stamp of approval, whether or not the relationship promotes mental health or personal growth.

In fact, some of the most pain-inflicting relationships are the most loyal, at least in some sense of the word. For some couples, the remorse, the professions of love, and even the passionate re-newal that follow ugly verbal or physical fights serve as relation-ship Super Glue. Nothing is more seductive than the tenderness of reconciliation. Yet the repeated wounds of conflicts may be very damaging to the self-esteem of one or both people in the re-lationship, resulting in permanent scars of cynicism and mistrust.

So yes, you want love. But make it a quest for good love, really good love. Love that not only has a strong foundation of loyalty, but love that makes you genuinely happy and promotes your emo-tional growth and personal evolution.

Cheating Yourself out of Love

If you have begun to believe that you are cheating yourself out of love, your first question is "Why have I done that?" The answer is simple: *for a good reason*. Human beings do not deprive themselves of love because they wish to be unhappy. They do not behave in self-defeating ways out of an inherent desire for isolation. You de-veloped your repertoire of attitudes and behaviors about love for reasons that made a great deal of sense *in the context in which they formed*.

Joyce, for instance, is a young woman who almost never dates at all. Occasional blind dates seem to go nowhere, and she is never spontaneously asked out by men she knows. Although her girl-friends like her, men are put off by her sarcasm and a certain toughness in her personality. Yet she's terribly lonely, especially at night, and increasingly spends her evenings with a box of Dou-bleStuf Oreos for comfort.

Obviously Joyce's toughness holds her back from love, and she herself knows it's a problem. But her personality developed as it did for a good reason. Joyce was raised in a large, boisterous fam-ily with three older brothers who teased her mercilessly. Her mother was too overwhelmed to intervene in the children's squabbles, and Joyce was left to deal with her brothers' venom on her own. Sarcasm and toughness were good emotional survival mechanisms, certainly much more helpful than bursting into tears every time she was teased.

Betsy's story is different. She started to date in her late teens and had several casual relationships in college. In her midtwenties Betsy fell in love with Tony, who was ten years older than she and had children from his first marriage. They dated for six years, and during the last several years she pressed him to get married several times. Each time, they weathered the crisis, Tony reassuring her of his love and his intention to marry when his kids got a little older and more settled. Then one day Betsy came to see him unexpectedly. In his bathroom wastebasket she found an empty panty-hose package—a brand that she had never used. After a tearful confrontation Tony confessed to his affair and admitted that he had begun to feel that he wanted to end the relationship with Betsy. She was devastated.

That was ten years ago. Betsy has not been in a serious relationship since Tony. She has remained frozen in her ability to love and trust again, and though she pays lip service to wanting to have a relationship, she does not make any serious effort to meet men.

If you are holding yourself back from love, your good reasons are probably some variation on the themes of Joyce and Betsy. At some period, or point in time, you felt the need to protect yourself from the vulnerability of love. Perhaps you experienced sustained assaults over a long period, through relationships at home or in school, that made you wall off your heart from further hurts. Or perhaps you experienced deep betrayal or disappointment once or more and began to believe that love was too risky a business to try again.

It's important to try to understand those experiences, and to compassionately acknowledge and accept the decisions you once made about love as simply the best way you knew to respond at the time. But it's even more important to be able to say: *That was then and this is now*. Make those words your mantra. The price you pay by remaining in a freeze-frame of old trauma is too enormous, too tragic. It's time to move on.

I once worked with a woman in therapy who was struggling to change an aspect of her emotional life. At one point she looked at me and said, "I've just got to change this. This is my one life, and I'm going to get to be dead for a long time."

I told that story to a friend who believes in reincarnation, and he said, "Well, I disagree. But it's because I believe I must prepare for the next life that I feel it's my responsibility to myself to live as fully as I can in this life."

So no matter what your philosophy of life is, you owe it to yourself to make the most of your time here on planet Earth. To allow one period of bad relationships to become the determining factor of everything else that ever happens to you may be understandable—but it's a terrible waste nonetheless.

Life on Both Sides

I've lived on both sides of the love fence. I married at twenty-one, went through medical school, residency, started my psychiatry practice, had two children, and was divorced at thirty-six. When I divorced, it quite literally never dawned on me that I would not quickly remarry, but in fact, I did not meet Jeb, the man who was to become my life partner, until I was forty-eight. Although I had several good dating relationships, I increasingly began to believe that I would never again find a soul mate, and that I would therefore never marry again.

Early on, though, I was struck by an image that stayed with me through the next twelve years. On my first Thanksgiving as a single person, I decided to fill my home with love and laughter by inviting all of my single friends for the feast. Thanksgiving morning, I began making the pumpkin pies. I kneaded the dough for the crust, rolled it out, and cut one perfect circle for the first pie. The sight of the remaining dough filled me with a sense of utter aloneness, for I was suddenly reminded of the loss of my one central relationship, my marriage. But I then gathered up the remaining bits and pieces, rolled them out, and made a second pie. The second pie looked rather homely, for there were cracks and crevasses where the bits were joined together. But when I served up both pies, they *tasted* just as good as each other, and the second pie was consumed with as much gusto as the first.

Love is like that. Of course you want that one, whole, perfect love that will meet all your needs and never desert you. Deprived of that love, you may forget that you can find bits and pieces of wonderfully loving relationships all around you—from family, friends, coworkers, people at church or other organizations, or even from small, simple moments in daily living. Every single person experiences that challenge: Will you retreat from life when you don't get that one perfect pie, or can you create and enjoy the richness of the second pie?

I truly loved that second pie during my long period of singlehood. Nonetheless, I understood myself well enough to recognize that I fundamentally wanted that one central relationship. I admit it, I have always been a happy little piggy at the trough of life, and I wanted the first *and* the second pie. So I had to search within get to the heart of the matter and to understand the issues that were holding me back from love.

Maybe you do, too.

You Have to Break a Rule

*To change your love life, you have to break
the psychological "rules" that are holding you back.*

Simply put, if your current strategies for finding love have been unsuccessful, you have to use new strategies to have better results. Whatever it is that you're doing, it isn't working. The passage of time has proven that, right? Why keep making the same mistakes over and over?

Each of us has a lengthy, detailed code of rules written deep within our unconscious minds that guides our behavior in matters of the heart. Your rule book determines to whom you will be attracted; how you will present yourself to that person; what your implicit and explicit expectations will be; what you are willing to give and what you expect to get; and so forth. If you repeatedly lose out in love, some of your rules need to be rewritten. Maybe they're in the section "Who Rings My Chimes?" Maybe it's later on, in "What Am I Willing to Invest in a Relationship?" Maybe it comes under "What Stresses Do I Get to Dump on the Schmo Who Tries to Love Me?"

The rule I had to change to find my relationship was simple, but it had had a profound impact on my life. It was under the section "How Much Discomfort and Frustration Am I Willing to Tolerate in a Relationship to Make It Work?" This section was actually quite short, for there was just one rule: NOT VERY MUCH. And while that rule made my life pleasant in the short run, on several occasions it had prevented me from developing deeper relationships. I had to change that rule to tolerate the frustrations of the long-distance relationship I began with Jeb, for it was really scary to fall in love with him when our future together was extremely uncertain. But then I *really* had to change that rule to leave my home and career in South Carolina and move to Maine to put our lives together.

If you're drawing a blank on which of your rules might be standing in the way of finding love, think about potential mates you know. Do you find yourself thinking:

"Lee's terrific, but I couldn't be married to someone who smokes."

"Terry's really neat, but I wouldn't want to have to deal with those kids from that first marriage."

"Shelley's been such a wonderful friend, but it would be tough to live with someone who is so messy."

"I really like Kyle, but I don't think I could stand living with a workaholic."

Perhaps your rule book contains prohibitions such as: No smokers. No kids or major baggage. Has to be neat. Can't be a workaholic.

All of those are good rules, no question about it. But the issue remains, whatever your rules are, are they worth the price of a life without love?

You alone can answer that question.

Maintaining "Good Love" in a Long-Term Relationship

As challenging as it is to be aware of your rule book for starting a relationship, it's even more challenging to be aware of the gazillions of rules you unconsciously impose when your relationship becomes permanent. The rules cover every breathing moment of your relationship, and they define what does and doesn't happen in your love life. Most importantly, they determine what the relationship feels like to you and your other.

People fall in love in a thrilling storm of attraction, lust, and excitement. Once that storm has passed, however, people *remain* in love for a simple reason: they like the way their other makes them feel.

Psychiatrists use a word, *affect*, to describe those moment-by-moment feelings that you experience in the course of the day. *Mood* is the emotional climate you experience over a period of days, weeks, and months, while *affect* is the much more fluid, reactive emotional coloration of the moment. *Affect* isn't commonly used in lay language, but it describes a really important aspect of how people relate.

Think about each friendship or relationship you have, and you'll be quickly aware that each one has a distinct affective profile. You probably have a few friends who reliably make you laugh. Maybe you have a family member who makes you feel guilty, anxious, or worried. Perhaps you have work associates who make you feel bored and flat, or an in-law who makes you feel withdrawn. All of those are feelings triggered by subtle aspects of your interaction.

What's more, you'll observe that in time your affective response to an individual begins to take on a life of its own. When you know someone well, he or she hardly has to say or do anything to trigger a cascade of feelings. Maybe all your mother-in-law has to do is walk in the room to make you feel irritated. Or perhaps all your best friend has to do is roll her eyes to make you start to laugh. Your affective reaction to an individual becomes an ingrained reaction that is difficult to change, even when you try hard. That's why it's so hard to refall in love with someone you've fallen out of love with.

Just as you react to others, others are reacting to you with affects triggered by your behavior. You do this in two ways. First, feelings are contagious. If you are happy, you will make others happy just by your presence. If you're anxious or depressed, those feelings will also infect others. The feelings you engender in oth-

ers will not be as strong as your own. But like whiffs of perfume—
or sour body odor—they can influence whether your other is
turned on or off by you. Take a moment and think about what
your typical emotional state is throughout the day; that's what
you're making other people feel, too.

The second, more powerful way is by specific interactions with
your other. The things you say and do, as well as the things you
don't say or don't do, all trigger emotions in others. That's a no-
brainer, right? But what's so hard to appreciate is your repetitive
pattern of subtle responses, postures, and behaviors *that are unconsciously determined and communicated.* It's challenging enough to become aware of the explicit things you say in a relationship, for at
least you can think a moment about your words before they leave
your mouth. What's harder, though, is to become sensitive to the
slew of behaviors that you never even consciously scrutinize. Two
categories of behavior are especially challenging: sins of omission
and nonverbal behaviors.

Why Are Sins of Omission So Destructive?

As you learn about the essential behaviors of good love and
sharpen your observations of how you react in relationships, I will
repeatedly call your attention to the things you *neglect* to do—*sins
of omission.* If you have trouble finding someone to love, you are
not fully aware of all the opportunities for connection you let slip
through your fingers, and you'll never even know what you've
missed. If you are in a relationship, you may not be aware of all
the tiny behaviors you're *not* engaging in that might really build a
stronger love. It's relatively easy to observe big, obvious things
you do to damage love. It's so much harder to become aware of
the relationship "glue" you're *not* creating. You rationalize why
you act the way you do, without asking the really important ques-

tion: *Yes, but at the end of the day is my behavior "working?" Is it bringing me the love I want?*

Listen to the words of Clem as he described why he bailed out of his relationship with Leigh:

"I've dated a lot of girls, and Leigh was a really sweet girl. We had some good times together. But there just wasn't enough—I don't know, chemistry, or electricity, or something—to keep it together.

"Part of it was that she was always sort of low-key. Like, if I suggested we do something, like go to a game or a movie, she'd never be really enthusiastic about it. We could go to a great movie, and I'd want to talk about it afterward, but she never really wanted to get into it. She'd always change the subject and want to talk about something practical.

"But the thing that was really hardest for me was that I never really knew what she was thinking. She was extremely quiet and kept a lot to herself. I don't think it was the quietness itself that bothered me, but the fact that I felt like it was just hard to know what was going on inside her."

Clem wasn't talking about bad things that Leigh did—he was talking about what she *didn't* do. When people talk to me about why their relationships fail, they speak of the acts of omission at least as often as the acts of commission. I hear:

"She just was so unaffectionate."

"He just didn't have much of a sense of humor or willingness to have fun."

"She seemed uncomfortable around my friends."

"He just lacked spontaneity. Everything had to be planned."

"She just seemed so unmotivated in her life."

Acts of omission are difficult to grasp because they are more unconscious in origin than acts of commission. They may pervade your relationship, but it is much harder for you and your lover to talk acts of omission than the tangible problems you have. It may literally never dawn on you that you are leaving out a vital nutrient of a relationship unless your lover is able to tell you. And if your fundamental problem is not having a relationship at all, it's especially important to address what you *don't* do that keeps you alone.

Why Are Nonverbal Behaviors More Powerful in Love than Verbal Behaviors?

Nonverbal behaviors are all the ways you communicate in relationships that do not involve talking. They include behaviors such as how and where you sit in the room when your other is present, and whether you make eye contact or laugh at his jokes. But they also include such things as how you decide to spend your free time, whether you initiate sex, and whether you remember and respect your other's likes and dislikes.

The vast majority of interactions are communicated nonverbally, rather than verbally. The challenge is that others are far more aware of your nonverbal messages than you are; the unconscious mind never really sleeps, and we are constantly communicating to others our real feelings. Further, when others are disturbed by our nonverbals, it is often difficult to address the problem up front. Your other might feel silly saying something like "I hate it that you make poor eye contact with me" or "Your body odor signals to me that you don't want to be close." But even if others don't address the issue with you, they react to your nonverbal cues.

Many affects contribute to the erosion of love, but anger, tension, and guilt are the royal three that are particularly damaging. Jean described how chronic guilt killed her friendship with Marge:

"Marge and I were great friends for a long time, really we were.

We would have such a blast together, and there was a long period of time when we were inseparable.

"But then I just started having less time for our friendship. I had started dating Jeff, so that made me less available, and work was pretty demanding, too. So instead of seeing Marge once or twice a week, it went to once or twice a month. I know that was hard on her, but realistically, what was I supposed to do? Dump Jeff so that I could stay friends with Marge?

"But I knew it was an issue, and so I tried to keep contact by calling her frequently and making sure that we saw each other every couple of weeks. But then she started guilt-tripping me. Nothing big, but whenever she'd answer the phone I'd hear this sad little 'hello.' This tragic little voice. And she wouldn't call me, but when I called her, she'd say something like 'Well, I haven't heard from you for a while.' And so I'd apologize, because I really did feel guilty.

"But then one weekend I called her and she didn't call back. On Monday she e-mailed me, and I was busy but I e-mailed back just a couple of lines. So then she e-mailed back this note: 'Well, so kind of you to surface for a moment.' That did it for me. I knew that if I confronted her, she'd tell me I was making a big deal over nothing, that it was just a joke—and I'm sure it was. But I just got so tired of feeling guilty *every single time* we had contact that I just withdrew completely."

On the Horns of a Dilemma

So here's the question you face as you begin to think more carefully about your love relationships. If the "devil" of relationships is in the "details" of tiny, repetitive behaviors, is the solution to become more vigilant about your every move, your every breath? *Of course not.* The best and happiest relationships are the most spontaneous. You want to be more free to be yourself, after all, not more self-conscious about your every move, right? So how in the world do you improve the way you interact with loved ones without becoming paralyzed by self-scrutiny?

Answer: By developing your ability to practice the Five Essentials of healthy loving. The Essentials target the underlying themes and issues that organize your behavior and emotional responses. While the Essentials are a set of specific behaviors you can begin to practice right away, they work from the outside in to change fundamental ways you think about yourself and your relationships. It's impossible to practice the Essentials without challenging basic ways that you think about love. And as you evolve in your capacity to love, your unconscious mind will automatically begin to reprogram the tiny nonverbal ways you interact with others.

It all starts with *engagement*, the first Essential. *Engagement* is a way of approaching your relationships that emphasizes loving interest in, rather than ownership of, your other. It's the simplest of all behaviors, and yet it is the most precious gift you can give another human.

CHAPTER TWO

Engage with the World around You

YOU MAY BELIEVE that getting to the heart of the matter and building the life you want will be a gradual, imperceptible process. In fact, you can *immediately* improve the quality of your daily life by focusing on just one small piece of your personality: your capacity to *engage* with others. Because that ability determines the vitality of your relationships, it's a key building block to getting the life you want.

Think, for a moment, of how variable the trait of "engageability" is in people you know. Those who connect easily are not necessarily smarter, funnier, or more beautiful than those who do not. In fact, a *lack* of pretentiousness is important for genuine engagement. But people who engage deeply approach their relationships with a particular mind-set. *They are open.* Open to find out about you, open to be surprised by what they learn, open to let you know them.

A couple of years ago I had the good fortune to be on the *Oprah Winfrey Show*. Oprah is said to be the most popular and successful woman in America, and I learned a great deal just by watching her up close for an hour. She opened the show by telling the story of her pedicurist, and she had the camera zoom in for a close up of the French pedicure that adorned her toes. Her feet, I noticed, looked a lot like mine, sporting a craggy landscape of bunions, corns, and even a blister or two. Was she self-conscious? Oh, no— because she was Oprah! Further, it was because *every* person out there could think, "Hey! Her feet look just like mine!" that she was able to connect with her audience.

Oprah is undoubtedly bright and attractive, and yet many people are equally bright and attractive. Her true genius is her ability to engage. She is delighted to reveal herself intimately to you and 24 million of her dearest friends. When you are with her, she appears fascinated by *you* and what makes *you* tick. Because there is so little emotional barrier between her and the audience, the TV screen that comes between you is a trifling matter.

Many, maybe most, people who attain great public popularity share that trait of Oprah's. Whether or not you agree with his politics or personal life, Bill Clinton is surely one of the most charismatic personalities of our age. Those who have met him always comment on the quality of instant engagement he makes with anyone, anytime, anyplace. Think of your own favorite politicians, entertainers, or public figures. You like them because they somehow resonate with you.

Engagement is an active process, a leap into the river of connection with other people. It's life in the here and now. You're not holding back out of shyness or snootiness. You're not brooding about past injustices, nor are you boring others by moaning about how much better life used to be. You're not postponing the happiness of today by banking on tomorrow.

When you engage more richly, you instantly deepen your capacity to love and be loved. You reveal yourself to others, allowing them to latch onto something within you that they can truly care about. You encourage them to reveal themselves to you, and you discover things worthy of your admiration. You begin to "play" with others in humor, creativity, and conversation, and your inter-actions become more fun. Importantly, you make it easier for peo-ple to love you, for people who engage are irresistibly magnetic to others.

The Wrapping Paper or the Gift?

Peruse the covers of women's magazines, and you will instantly see the extraordinary attention women pay to the externals: breast size, hip size, makeup, hairstyles, fashions, accessories. We paint our lips, bleach our teeth, streak our hair, pierce our skin, and may even tattoo our bodies, all in an attempt to attract men. And those efforts do pay off . . . a little. As humans we are visual creatures, and males are undoubtedly attracted to, *okay*, attractive women. But attraction is not the same as attachment. The vast majority of first dates do not lead to an enduring romance, much less a com-mitted relationship. Simply put, there is a big difference between admiring the wrapping paper and wanting to keep the gift.

Ladies, listen up, please, I have real news: the majority of men are not actually so dumb as we think. They actually are turned off by vanity—just as we are. They're not any more excited about a woman who is preoccupied with her buff body than you are in search of a man obsessed with his own big muscles. They are gen-erally far more forgiving of your having a few extra pounds than you are. They may admire a new dress, but what they love is the woman inside the dress.

I know these things because I have listened carefully to what males say about females. I've been a fly on the wall when my college-age son and his friends talk about girls. They don't talk about boob size, but they are contemptuous of girls who seem fake or dishonest. They're quite sensitive to being used by girls to enhance their self-esteem or social prestige. They may hook up with a good-looking girl, but they hold on to the ones with character and good hearts.

I've listened to my male friends, colleagues in the medical world in which I've lived, as they talk about their marriages. They get burned out on high-maintenance women. They're at peace in their marriages when their wives are mostly happy, busy with their own lives, and are able to make them feel appreciated as husbands. What men hate the most is when they feel that their wives are "insatiable"—that no matter what happens, no matter what they do, it's never quite enough.

And most importantly, I've listened to my male patients talk about their girlfriends or wives. On any number of occasions, I've heard a man describe his wife as "beautiful" and then been surprised when I meet a woman who is actually quite plain. But I'm impressed that men are really quite perceptive about a woman's insides—her character, her inner peace, and her capacity to deeply engage with those she loves. They are aware of the difference between one who demands attention and one who deserves attention.

So, yes, pay a bit of attention to your wrapping paper, for that may affect whether the gift is picked up off the shelf. But really focus on the gift itself—the you that engages with your other.

Attention Deficit Relationship Disorder

The curse of modern living surely is that an infinite number of distractions keep us from really paying attention to our relationships. Pressures of work, the turn-on/turn-off entertainment of televisions and computers, and the fatigue of daily responsibilities, all compete quite successfully for the energy and attention we should be investing in our human world.

Yet even more distracting than your external environment is

the steady bombardment of distractions that come from within you. The next time you are in a conversation with someone you love, monitor your thoughts. What are you thinking about as your other is talking? Are you really paying attention, or are you thinking about how to end the conversation? Are you absorbing each thought he is sharing, or are you busy formulating your own response, waiting for a moment to interrupt? Do you change the subject or let him continue? Do you ask the questions that signal a deep interest in what he is saying?

Several years ago, I was leading a seminar for psychiatry residents at the medical school where I worked. As I lectured, I noticed something comical. I knew they were pretty bored; to be honest, I was even boring myself, a bad sign. But as I made eye contact with each of them, they would automatically begin to nod their heads as if affirming whatever I was droning on about at the moment. In the midst of my scholarly pontification, I became distracted by the thought that I could telepathically will each of my students to bob his or her head just by looking at him or her. Suddenly they looked to me like those little bobbleheads that people put on their dashboard, and I burst out laughing. (*That* got their attention.) In time, I realized something interesting: when what I was saying was truly provocative, they didn't head-bob—they were listening too actively. They might be agreeing and actively thinking about the implications of what I was saying. They might be disagreeing and trying to formulate a challenge. Only when they had really tuned me out did they put themselves into an automatic state of seeming agreement, a trick they had learned through their many years of formal education.

One of the signs that you may be suffering from attention deficit relationship disorder is that you find yourself in that automatic-pilot, head-bobbing, fogged-out state. Perhaps your version is the empathic grunt, though you aren't really sure what you are grunting about. Maybe you've learned to compose your face in a caring, sympathetic way, even when your eyes are glazed and your mind is in another galaxy, far, far away. Wake up! Turn on a light inside you that will burn off that fog so you can really see, really hear, your other. As the clouds lift, your other will be able to really see and hear you as well. You'll begin to engage.

Learning to Engage

Think of all the things you learned as a child. Your parents probably taught you about politeness, obedience, and discipline. Your schoolteachers taught you English, math, history, and a myriad of other subjects. At your place of worship you learned about your faith. But did anyone ever take the time to teach you how to engage? Probably not, because we assume that it's just an inborn personality trait. You either have it or you don't.

Wrong! Of course you can improve your ability to engage. It's only a set of behaviors motivated by the genuine desire to live more fully in the human world. If you have the desire, you can easily learn the behaviors . . . and open yourself up to an exchange of love.

When people attempt to improve their relationships, they usually try to be more likable—in other words, they try to get others to like *them*. Try, instead to do the opposite: focus your energy on trying to like, and even love, your other better. Mutual liking is the driving energy of engagement, and that energy can begin within you.

All people yearn to be liked and are exquisitely sensitive to subtle cues about whether they are accepted and approved of. We signal our like or dislike of others in innumerable ways—eye contact, shifts in body posture, murmurs to signal listening—and it is difficult for you to fool another person about your feelings for long.

To really engage with others, you must begin from your "inside" out, increasing your capacity to genuinely like the people in your human world.

You will like an individual to the degree you can truly understand him or her. Every person has a kernel of humanity inside. Find that kernel, and you will understand your other's motivations and connect to lovable aspects of his character. Your goal is simply to try to understand your other. Merely trying to understand is a potent form of engagement.

Can *anyone* be liked through understanding? I suspect the answer is yes. A true story: A couple of years ago, I was on call for our psychiatric hospital for the weekend. It was a truly onerous job, because each day I had to speak with, write a brief chart note on, and review the medications of sixty inpatients. My goal was to "get through" each patient as efficiently as possible.

As always happened, there was one problem patient who had no intention of being "got through." He was behaving horribly on the unit—he ate some paper clips and had to be x-rayed, he was obnoxious and provocative with the other patients, and he would not comply with what the nurses asked. I curbed my irritation that my work was not going to go speedily and went to see him. I talked to him for some time, made a change or two in his medicines, then spoke to the nursing staff. I commented on his odd appearance and his deformed nose. What had happened?

"Oh," said the nurse, "his father cut it off with a pair of scissors when he was a child."

It is easy enough to dismiss someone you don't understand. But simply hearing "his side of the story" will transform your feelings, if you can open your heart up just a wee bit. It did mine.

The movie *In the Bedroom* reflects that understanding another human being alters your interaction even with those you hate. In the movie, the teenage son falls in love with a just-separated older woman, a mother of two. Her husband, a truly creepy, yuck-o character, murders the boy. You hate the murderer, honest to goodness you do. But then the boy's father, seeking revenge, takes the murderer hostage and they have to go into the murderer's home. In the house, you see several things that force you to understand him. You see his sons' childish drawings taped to the wall. You see a large photo of the murderer and his once loving, laughing wife hanging on the bathroom wall. Despite yourself you begin to understand why he committed the murder, and your hatred softens. You can't help yourself.

Engaging begins with simply trying to understand.

Understanding the Ones You "Know" Best

It's an old cliché that the married man who is propositioning a new woman says, "My wife just doesn't understand me." It's a cliché because often enough it's true, every bit as much as he doesn't understand her. Paradoxically, often the people you know the best are the ones you understand the least.

A classic paper in the psychoanalytic literature by W. R. Bion admonishes analysts to listen to their patients "without memory or desire." It's a counterintuitive suggestion, for therapists are trained to take detailed histories and to set defined goals. What Bion says, however, is that we often fail to really hear what others are saying because we are translating their words to fit with all of our preconceived ideas about them. Our "memory" prevents us from hearing them with freshness and keeps us from hearing what they are trying to communicate. Our "desire"— our own goals for that person or our interaction—blocks our helping them to gain the inner freedom to go in whatever direction they want. To paraphrase Frank Sinatra, we want others to "do it our way."

When "memory" dominates a long-term relationship—with your mate, your kids, sibs, or parents—you develop such ingrained expectations of your other's behavior and motivations that you're blind to new feelings that might be bubbling up. He or she perceives you turning a deaf ear to his true voice and shuts up. You, in turn, may be experiencing the reciprocal process. The relationship may go along quietly in that way, but each of you becomes gradually aware that your love has become stale. The signs are obvious in retrospect. You begin telling your most important secrets to someone else, maybe someone you haven't known very long. You shield your other from truths you fear would be hurtful. You notice your own responses becoming mechanical.

When "desire" dominates, you structure your responses to achieve a goal you have for the relationship. Perhaps you want to get married and your lover is ambivalent; you unconsciously find ways not to allow him to speak honestly, and you manipulate him into agreeing to more commitment than he feels. Maybe it's your child who is frightened by the goals you have set for him, but doesn't know how to tell you. You give him a pep talk every time he tries to explain his feelings, and he gradually shuts down.

Neglecting to invest the effort to truly understand your other is a nonverbal sin of omission that invisibly erodes your relationship. The realization of the damage you have inflicted may feel quite shocking, especially when you hear the accusation "You just don't understand me."

To really understand your other, imagine yourself stepping into his or her skin—and out of yours. Suspend disbelief. Stop thinking up counterarguments. Rather, imagine yourself experiencing everything your other has been through that has brought about his or her current point of view. Imagine hurting the way your other has been hurt. Imagine that your self-esteem has been forged by the victories your other has enjoyed. Imagine living in your other's human world. See the world through your other's eyes, hear it with your other's ears, and imagine yourself feeling your other's feelings.

Now you're in the mind-set of real engagement.

Engagement at Its Best

In its fullest, most intense form, engagement conveys a simple but extraordinary message:

I believe in you.

From the youngest of us to the oldest, the slowest to the smartest, the weakest to the strongest, each of us needs to hear the voice of someone who really believes in us. We need that voice when we've failed, to hear the encouragement that allows us to get back up on our feet. We listen for the voice when we've succeeded, for otherwise the awards podium is a lonely place. We need the comfort of the voice when we're floundering, for it reminds us of our inner reservoirs of strength. And we need the voice to admire our drive and ambition, to encourage us to turn our vision into action.

The deepest, most profound love relationships are based on the mutual, encompassing belief each person has in the totality of the other. But even more limited moments of engagement are meaningful because they convey a bit of belief. The coach puts his arm around the shoulder of the boy who blew the game when he missed that last free throw: *I believe in you.* The physical therapist touches the cheek of her patient and says, "You've been so strong, you've been through a lot." *I believe in you.* The man listens carefully and patiently to his date's description of her fears about not getting the job she's applied for: *I believe in you.*

For most people you meet, there is no need to convey false belief in the totality of that person—you don't even know the total- ity of the vast majority of the people you meet. But conveying your belief in whatever small part of them that is revealed is a pre- cious gift. You can reflect your appreciation of their courage as they relate a moment of anxiety. You can share their optimism for their future plans as their excitement spills out. You can laugh with them at their jokes, applauding their sense of humor. All of those are small acts of engagement, tiny seeds of love.

Terms of Engagement

If half of engagement is really listening, the other half is the active ways you respond—or choose not to respond. Each of us develops an emotional rule book I call the *terms of engagement*. Your terms are a set of rules that define the *how, who, what, where, when,* and *why* of your interactions with others. You originally developed your terms unconsciously—you can't probably even remember why or how you made the decisions you did about your rules. Nonetheless, they are all-important in shaping your ability to en- gage.

Your terms define what *doesn't* happen as much as they define what *does* happen in your daily life. They often exclude many wonderful experiences that could vastly enrich your life, and you never even realize what you are missing. They may prevent mo- ments of real insight you could have about the people you love best. While you are quite aware of the life you do live, you may not appreciate your "unlived life"—all the events and relation- ships that do not occur because of the way you have set your terms.

Some examples of terms that constrict your capacity to engage:

Work is primarily for the purpose of earning money. My goal is to earn as much money as quickly as I can, then get the hell out and go home. You've excluded the workplace as a place of love, enjoyment, and meaning; the experience of contributing in work is limited to earning money to support your family.

There's a time for play and a time for work. After school, the kids need to stop horsing around and get their work done. You've excluded homework as a time for fun in the sharing of jokes or learning through games or inventing funny ways to remember information. Your grim attitude makes your children want to withdraw from you; you've transmitted your tension to them, and they resent you for it.

I really dread my husband's family reunions. I know I have to go because it's expected, but I can't wait to get home. You hold your in-laws at arm's length and keep yourself from experiencing each of them as a separate, unique individual.

All of these are examples of *compartmentalization:* you create little boxes in your life in which you interact with others. But life doesn't come tied up in neat little packages. The people in your life may not like their compartments. They may not be willing or able to deliver up a dose of love or joy just because you're ready for it. They may decide to simply undo the latch and climb out of the box when your back is turned. You've set your terms in a way that impoverishes your life.

There is, in fact, only one way to change your human world: change your terms of engagement, which are the *how, who, what, where, when,* and *why* of your interactions. You may change any one of the six terms, or you may change all the terms. You may change the terms a lot or a little. But each change will have a profound impact on the quality of your life. Like Alice stepping through the looking glass, you will gain entry into a life that would otherwise have been unlived.

How

How to engage addresses the way you interact with another individual. It's actually quite simple. *You just show interest.*

What?! Plain old *interest? Interest* seems like such an ordinary, everyday commodity. But deep, genuine interest is one of the most valuable and rare gifts you can give another—and lack of interest is toxic to a relationship. You may have grown up with dutiful, responsible parents, yet felt unloved because your parents did not understand and appreciate your authentic wishes and feelings. You may be in a marriage that is stable and loyal, yet you and your husband have ceased to be invested in each other's inner world. You may be bonded but not engaged.

Interest is the fundamental building block of love, for nothing *feels* more like love than interest. Ninety percent of the healing power of psychotherapy lies in the fifty-minute experience of the therapist's genuine interest in the client. It is a sad commentary on human life that few of us receive a full fifty minutes once a week of unadulterated interest from another human being, and that is why therapy is so powerful. Yet patients regularly feel loved by their therapists and in turn may love their therapists back because they crave just having someone show interest.

The most precious type of interest is *nonjudgmental.* Interest in another person is truly loving when you accept their inner world without imposing your own values, standards, and expectations—a no-strings-attached engagement. Because our lives are so intertwined with those we love, it is hard to stay nonjudgmental with them; it is far easier to be nonjudgmental of someone whose life has little impact on yours. Yet conveying criticism of your other shuts down open communication, for it reflects that so-called love is heavily contaminated by self-interest.

Sally, a woman in her late twenties, called my attention to the importance of nonjudgmental interest in a rather simple story she told me. Sally worked as a nurse anesthetist and had recently moved in with her lover. Sally disliked her work, however, and had decided to become an acupuncturist. Her father was a surgeon and her mother was a nurse, and both were pillars of their small, conservative community. They were appalled by her decision to live with her lover and also disapproved of her decision to leave the world of traditional Western medicine to learn alternative medicine. "Why must they always pass judgment on me?" she asked despairingly. "Why can't they just *be interested*?"

Just be interested. Sally's parents would undoubtedly say—and feel—that they genuinely loved their daughter. They were convinced that Sally's adoption of their value system would lead to a more stable and rewarding life. Their sole interest was her long-term well-being, they would say. Yet Sally's experience of her parents was very different. She felt her parents experienced her as an extension of their self-esteem, not as a person whose autonomous values and goals they respected. Only if she conformed to their values was she a satisfactory reflection of themselves as parents.

Charlotte Brontë once said that morality should not be confused with conventionality. Likewise, loving engagement should not be confused with duty and responsibility. It is possible to feel commitment, duty, and responsibility to a child, spouse, parent, or friend without feeling liking, understanding, or affection—the ingredients of engagement. You can probably think of people who have demonstrated commitment to you while making you feel you've disappointed them. Nothing is more painful than when someone who claims to love you doesn't even really *know* you! The fullest possible relationship offers both the deep interest of loving engagement *and* the abiding work of true loyalty and commitment.

It is extremely easy to become so impressed by your sense of responsibility that you neglect engaging. A personal story: When my children were small, I dutifully set aside time every day to read to them. In retrospect, I recognize that I became somewhat mind-numbed after years of Dr. Seuss and the Berenstain Bears; I could chant "One-fish-two-fish-red-fish-blue-fish" while having an out-of-body experience. One Christmas, however, my daughter's great-aunt came to visit and brought with her a scratch-and-sniff book. I recall watching her read the book to Stephanie:

"Oh, look, let's scratch that one. It's supposed to be raspberry jam. What do you think? I think it smells like raspberries. Mmm, yum, yum, yum. Oh, look, now the bears have gone into the kitchen to taste Mama's spaghetti sauce. Let's smell that one. Do you like that? I don't think that one really smells so much like spaghetti." The two of them were deeply absorbed together in sniffing and scratching, scratching and sniffing. Both of them were fascinated with the book; *they were truly engaged*. My aunt had immersed herself in the mind of a three-year-old, exploring the world of smells. Loving engagement is nothing more—or less—than a collection of such moments.

Not infrequently in couples therapy I will hear couples confuse duty and loyalty for loving engagement:

CECILIA *(tragically)*: I don't feel like you really love me.

JASON: (grunt)

CECILIA *(becoming more shrill)*: Aren't you going to respond?

JASON *(defensively)*: Whaddya mean, I don't love ya? I married ya, didn't I?

Yet, while many women can relate to the feeling that their husband is there-but-not-there, it is more challenging to own up to the deadening impact of *their own* emotional detachment. In private, Cecilia related to me how disconnected she was from her husband during lovemaking. Cecilia felt it was "important for the marriage" to have sex once a week and would present the opportunity to her husband with some regularity. Absent from their lovemaking, however, was any interest in romance, pleasure in Jason's eroticism, or curiosity about what he was experiencing. Cecilia was carrying out her wifely duty and even experienced orgasm, but was decidedly unengaged in the emotional experience of lovemaking. Small wonder that Jason, too, detached from her. Theirs was a dutiful but unengaged marriage.

The problem with becoming overly impressed by your sense of duty is that it lets you off the hook from tough questions about your capacity to love. If you are a Jason with your whaddya-mean brand of love, you might wonder: What is the danger of truly engaging with Cecilia? Might it mean that you would have to acknowledge your contribution to her unhappiness? Might you be challenged to be less selfish, more egalitarian in the home, more sensitive to how she is feeling? If you are a Cecilia, you might have to ask yourself: Why have you turned off your sexual interest in Jason? Is it your way of punishing him? Is it because you're scared to relinquish your need to control by engaging intimately and erotically? Might it be that you see him primarily as a provider, rather than as a human being with his own needs and sensibilities?

If you realize that love is demonstrated by showing interest, you quickly realize that you can engage in loving behaviors anytime, anyplace, and with any person. You can express interest in a baby in a stroller at the grocery store, the person sitting next to you on the subway, or the fellow fan cheering for the home team in the next seat. Your life will be richer for those tiny interactions, and the simple experiences of daily living will become more fun.

You may be lulled into thinking that this business of showing interest is really pretty easy—until you turn to your most intimate relationships and realize how difficult, even painful, the experience of interest can be. Unlike the casual stranger you strike up a conversation with, enduring friendships require you to share experiences that range from joyful and exciting to horrifying and depressing. You may *talk* about difficult experiences with a stranger, but you actually *share* the difficulty with those whom you love. Sometimes just the sharing of pain—scary as it may be—can be the ultimate act of engagement.

Sarah, a caller to my radio show, reflected this. Her best friend, Maria, had lost her only daughter, a young woman, in an auto accident several months previously. To make matters more horrible, the young woman had been nine months pregnant, and Maria had witnessed the terrible event. As she described her friend's pain, Sarah's own voice was heavy with grief and despair. Though not actively suicidal, Maria had lost the will to live. She was unable to continue working as a teacher, unable to care about anything in her daily life, and unwilling to believe that life had meaning for her any longer. Sarah tried to remind Maria that her daughter would have wanted her to go on living and experience life's pleasures again, but Sarah's words had little effect on her friend.

As Sarah spoke, I was reminded of the story years ago of little Jessica, a small girl in Texas who was trapped in a well for several days while workers dug a second well to rescue her. As she lay trapped, loving adults talked to her through microphones, offering comfort and reassurance during her terrifying ordeal. While they themselves were not extricating her, their words of encouragement undoubtedly helped her emotionally to survive the trauma she was experiencing.

And so I suggested to Sarah not to underestimate that *just being present* with Maria while she was in the deep well of despair was enormously important for her survival. To try too vigorously to pull her out of the well before she was ready would only increase her pain; she would gradually leave on her own when she was able. The most loving thing Sarah could do was to show deep interest in what Maria was experiencing—to allow her to voice her despair, outrage, and hopelessness. It would be terribly painful to maintain interest in Maria's feelings during the months and years of her grief. Sarah would be tempted to do what all of us do when we see others suffer: we offer advice, try to lighten the mood, tell stories about our own pain, or suggest ways to "move on." But however well-meaning those ministrations are, they leave the bereaved person alone in the well.

Authentic interest is easy to demonstrate when discussing your nephew's plans for law school, your coworker's wedding preparations, or your husband's latest promotion. But what about responding to Aunt Helen's description of her bouts with constipation, your best friend's laments about her zillionth argument with her philandering boyfriend, or your niece's description of her latest tattoo? The icky feelings stirred up within you—boredom, irritation, distaste—all shut down your interest. You will try a variety of maneuvers to reestablish the interaction on *your* terms, thus disengaging from an authentic experience of the other.

The Liberation of "Just" Listening

As a therapist who spends many hours each week "just" listening to people tell me their problems, I'm often asked questions like "How can you stand it? Don't you find it draining? Don't you take it home with you and worry about your patients?"

The answer is no, I rarely find therapy sessions draining. When I'm not with my patients, I do think about them at times, particularly if I'm puzzled by their diagnosis or not sure what direction to go with their treatment. But I never worry about my patients be-

cause I always believe that they will get better. Incidentally, I'm
not always right about that—not all patients do get better, for a
variety of reasons. But as I'm sitting with them, I image in my
mind how they might feel and behave if they got well, and I feel
optimistic.

I feel true responsibility to be the best doctor I can be for my
patients, but I never believe I can "fix" them. That they have to do
for themselves. One can provide sun, water, and soil for a plant,
but the plant has to do its own growing.

Likewise, when you're responding to a friend or lover who has
a problem you'd love to fix for them, remember that *it's impossible
to help another more than he is able to help himself.* It's just not in your
power to "make it all better." Further, when you take over, you
convey a very mixed message: *I'll fix this for you because I love you
(and because I don't really think you're capable of fixing it yourself).* Or,
*I'll give you some great advice (because I don't really think you're smart
enough to figure it out for yourself).* Smart therapists are slow to give
advice because people rarely follow it and it spares us the embarrassment of being ignored. We know our clients will end their bad
relationships, switch jobs, decide to marry, or confront their
coworker when they're good and ready, and not a moment before.
Our goal is to enable our clients to give themselves good advice.
On the other hand, communicating the simple thought *I believe in
you* empowers them to greet their problems with energy and confidence.

Once you begin to engage rather than tune out; to listen rather
than fix; to express confidence in your other rather than take over
his or her life—you will feel liberated to really enjoy your relationships. You'll wake up less often in the middle of the night
worrying about someone else's life. You won't agonize over
whether you said the right thing to your best friend or call her up
with just one more piece of advice. You won't immerse yourself in

other people's problems as a defense against dealing with your own problems. You'll feel free—free at last!

Who

Your innate tendency will always be to look toward people who are like you as candidates for engagement. A little duckling imprints from whatever it sees when it first blinks its newborn eyes, but you will always be attracted to people who remind you of other people in your life. Those people may or may not be like *you*; the duckling, after all, will follow a human if that's the first thing available to it.

Seeking the familiar "who" is a double-edged sword. Relatively greater emotional safety comes from staying within your tribe. You know what to do, how to act, and what to expect. You feel protected from the unexpected. But that's the problem, isn't it? It's possible to be so safe that nothing new, startling, exciting, and stimulating ever happens in your life. You're not stretched to grow and adapt. As your life proceeds, your range of experience becomes increasingly telescoped. You become a psychological dinosaur: perfectly adapted to your specific environment, unable to evolve when the climate changes.

Further, you may reach a point when you realize you've been plopped down into the wrong tribe. Maybe the family you were born into just isn't the right fit for you, but you choose friends and lovers like your parents anyway because they make you feel at home—for better or worse. Maybe you find yourself at a school or in a neighborhood or caught up with a church or company or organization that isn't really you, or at least not the "you" you want to be. It's time to reach out of the tribe . . . to reach toward the unfamiliar.

Your terms of engagement about "who" are unique to you.

Take a moment and jot down some notes on your hitherto unwritten rules of "who." You may have rules that limit your interaction with others based on:

- Appearance

- Age

- Gender

- Occupation

- Social class

- Education

- Money

- Interests

- Life goals

- Potential for matrimony

Your rules exist in the interface of your conscious and unconscious minds. You don't think about them consciously most of the time, but you can become aware of the rules if you give it a little thought. You may find that you have defined your terms so narrowly that hardly anyone gets into your inner circle.

Roger is an example of someone who did just that. Three years ago he had moved to our city and was baffled about why he was having trouble finding a new relationship. No one seemed really right. He had just spent the whole Christmas holiday alone, and he was tired of feeling so isolated.

"Roger," I said, "let's put the issue of romantic love aside for a moment. What about developing friendships with some of your business friends, so at least you'd have some steady, reliable friends for support and fun?"

"Oh, I've never really been one to have a drink with the guys. Men just don't do much for me. Yeah, I can shoot the breeze for a while, but it's not like having a girlfriend."

"Okay, Roger, but you might meet some appropriate women through the wives of your male friends."

"Well, I guess, but the few times that's happened, they're just not right. They're usually too old, like around my age. I really like younger women."

"But I thought you'd been going out with a younger woman. Why didn't that work out?"

"Yeah, I've gone out with lots of younger women. But usually they've been married and have kids, and I don't want to raise someone else's kids. Or they want to get married and have kids, and I just don't want to go through that."

"Roger, where do you go to meet women, then? It seems like you're asking for a younger woman, but someone who has something in common with you, so where would you be likely to find someone like that?"

"Well, now you've hit on the problem. The only place I know of is bars, and I've met some nice ladies in bars. But then it's like they're too eager, and some of them aren't too bright, and I get turned off."

As we talked on, I realized that just looking at statistical probability, Roger had a big problem with the "who" of his terms of engagement. Because he really had no interest in friendships with men, he had written off half of the world's population. Out of the female world, he was only interested in good-looking single women available for romance . . . bye-bye to another 47 percent. Then there was the age requirement—she had to be between twenty-five and forty (Roger was fifty-five)—so now we were down to maybe 1 percent of the world's population. But of that group, she couldn't have any of the pesky complications of life, such as children of her own or health or financial problems. Oh, and did I mention she also had to be bright, well-spoken, and educated? And remember that she had to hang out in bars at night, because that was the only place Roger ever went to look for women. So because there just didn't seem to be any childless, healthy, beautiful, educated, young female barflies interested in fifty-five-year-old men, Roger was alone.

Roger was extreme. The size of his unlived life was as big as God's outdoors, for his terms shut him out of the human world almost entirely. He lived in his secret self with his brilliant, nubile, mature, childless, thirty-year-old, bar-hoppin' girlfriend, but she never appeared in his human world. Yet each of us has a bit of Roger in us, turning our backs on many wonderful opportunities for friendships, associations, or even just small, delightful conversations that might add richness to our daily life.

What are your rules? Do you exclude people because they don't look quite like what you'd imagined, or because you've established a set of mutually contradictory requirements? Or are you so busy looking for that perfect soul mate that you turn away from casual friendships that might bring you enjoyment and enrichment?

One way of expanding your terms is to change those rules. Another is what I call the "10 percent stretch": with each person you meet in the day, stretch the interaction just a bit further than you might be inclined to. Find out something about the retail clerk you might otherwise not chat with. Have lunch with the person you've been sitting with at your son's games but have never gotten to know really well. Take some time with the coworker from the other side of the hall and let her know something personal about you . . . and ask her something personal about herself. Express some warmth—a moment of love. Tell a joke—a moment of fun.

What

What is a concrete but all-important term of engagement. Specifically, once you have determined the *who, what* do you allow into your relationship? What do you talk about, and what are the things that you consciously and unconsciously choose not to talk about? Do you keep your interactions superficial, or do you connect with others through conversation about things you really care about? Do you open the door for the possibility of love?

At any given moment in a conversation, you have two fundamental choices. You can try to just "get through" the conversation, sticking to neutral, meaningless topics. Alternatively, you can allow the conversation to create a shared understanding between you and your other about issues you really enjoy or care about.

People commonly avoid the emotional honesty of real connection with others in numerous ways. One of the most common ways is by presenting oneself as an always-happy, in-control person, surely the most dishonest of all facades. An acquaintance I'll call Chris exemplified this. Raised to be "well-bred," she was taught early on that it was impolite to talk too much about herself. In conversations she went out of her way to show attentiveness to others, asking many questions and showing great interest in their lives. As a result, people liked Chris. Yet no one really *knew* Chris. When she did talk about herself, she displayed only squeaky-clean feelings, refusing to say anything bad about anyone else, certainly never gossiping, and revealing little of the ornery emotions—fear, irritation, jealousy, boredom, or dislike—that are normal, natural, and funny parts of the human experience. On the surface she seemed very engaged because she was a great listener; but she held back from true emotional honesty. Over time in her relationships, her lack of self-revelation made other people hold back, and interactions with Chris remained shallow.

Another extreme: Pat was a wonderful eccentric, an inventor whose bachelor pad was a little shop of wonders. Gregarious and witty, Pat had a charisma and charm that made people want to be let into his inner circle. Yet Pat rarely asked his friends about themselves; the interactions were always about his offbeat ways, his funny stories about himself, and his caustic and hilarious perceptions. Yes, he engaged with others, but again the engagement was shallow because he displayed little curiosity about the lives of his friends.

John, a third extreme, was an intellectual, bright and interested in a huge array of subjects. Politics, science, and art were only a few of the areas that occupied his mind. He, too, was a wonderful conversationalist, although talking to him made me feel my intellect was in the "dull–normal" range. But John didn't talk about himself or show much interest in the inner world of others—he avoided the interpersonal connection of the world Martin Buber called "I-Thou." He, too, had terms of engagement that severely limited the depth of connection in his relationships.

People who engage most deeply and successfully do so in the three arenas of conversation. They reveal themselves, allowing themselves to be loved and enjoyed. They show deep interest in the lives of others, searching for something to appreciate. And finally, they are interested in issues "out there," finding topics of mutual interest to play with in conversation, like kids climbing into a sandbox to build a castle together. They search to find a bit of meaning in each conversation, rather than settling for empty formalities.

Just as there is an unlived life, there are also infinite unspoken conversations, consisting of all of the things that might have been said if you had only engaged with your other. At each moment of conversation you have choices—to reveal yourself honestly, to explore something about the other person, or to search for a shared experience. The quality of the engagement you experience is defined by the *what* of your terms of engagement.

Where

If you're in a relationship already, the *where* of engaging with your other is simple—anywhere, anytime. If you're not in a relationship but you're trying to meet someone, the answer is still simple: *You can engage anywhere except when you are squirreled away alone within your own home, hunkered down with the phone off the hook.*

I repeat: anywhere but within your own home. The chances of a special stranger walking up to your front door and ringing that bell are remote. You have to get out of the house and really reach out.

Here's how it happened for me. My sister Barbara met her husband, Clark, on an airplane. Clark was from Rochester, Minnesota. Barbara was flying home from visiting me and struck up a conversation with the guy next to her—the guy to whom she's now been married for fifteen years, the father of her three children. So Barbara always said to me, "Linda, if you get on a plane, look nice. You never know."

So a few years ago, at the sprightly age of forty-eight and after many years of singlehood, I indeed found myself putting on a nice suit to get on a plane to go to a medical meeting. A handsome stranger did indeed get on the plane, but much to my disappointment was not assigned to the seat next to me. Nonetheless, when the flight was over we got onto the same shuttle bus to get back to the terminal. The stranger and I struck up a conversation.

He was from Rochester, Minnesota. *Omigod!*

Further, we were going to the same meeting and staying at the same hotel. We learned that we had gone to the same medical school, knew the same people, and had the same job at our respective schools. He had graduated from medical school in the same ceremony I had graduated from college—twenty-six years earlier. His son and my daughter had both attended the same tiny college in Vermont. We decided to share a taxi to our hotel and later decided to share the rest of our lives together.

So the moral of this story is that if you want to find true love, ride around on airport shuttle buses. Or talk to a stranger at the hardware store or the bookstore or Wal-Mart. Or volunteer to help out at the next Race for the Cure or take a sailing class. Ask your friends to set you up or try a dating service. Just get out of the house, please.

When

Like *where*, *when* is also a simple multiplier: to double your engagement, double the amount of time in which you allow engagement to occur. To double your chances of meeting someone interesting, double the amount of time you are available for engagement. Yet it may be even harder to modify *when* than *where*. Defining *when* you engage is fundamentally a control issue, and the substance you are trying to control is your time.

Jill described to me the challenge of expanding *when* on a recent bike ride with her friend Louise. It was a glorious day, and the hill they were climbing felt like just the right amount of challenge. "All's right with the world," mused Jill. Suddenly Louise veered off the road and down a driveway—she had spotted some friends of hers and wanted to stop and say hi. Jill's heart sank. Knowing that the bike ride was over for the afternoon, she went into the friends' home to sit on the back porch and drink iced tea. Yet in a few minutes she realized the friends were really special people; she soon found herself engaged in an absorbing conversation about their shared interests. At the end of the visit the friends invited her and Louise to a party later in the month, and in time the friendship deepened—in turn leading to other friendships and social opportunities.

For Jill the challenge of engagement was the *when* of the inter-action. Had she and Louise met the friends for a preplanned restaurant dinner, she would have been fine; it was being pulled off her agenda for the afternoon that was difficult. Yet Louise's spontaneous friendliness generally made her far more open to en-gagement than Jill was. Engagement, after all, isn't only a matter of when *you* decide you're ready to engage—it's also about when someone in your path is willing to engage with you.

It is a wonderful paradox of human living that the harder you try to package your life neatly and attractively, the less fulfilling it becomes. The more you try to control, the less of value there is to control. It's in the mess of living—the surprises, accidents, chance encounters, waylaid plans—that the real wonder of expe-rience occurs.

Why

The *why* of your terms addresses what you hope to get from the interaction with your other. As you're reading, you may be think-ing of many reasons for improving your ability to engage. Perhaps you'd like to find someone to marry, and you'd like to be able to connect more comfortably with potential candidates. Maybe you feel that your children are withdrawing from you, and you'd like to strengthen your relationships with them. You might realize that you could be more successful in the workplace if you interacted more comfortably. Or perhaps you'd like to enlarge your circle of friends.

All of those are worthy reasons and comprise an excellent set of ulterior motives for engagement. I'd suggest, though, that it's best to put those motives on the back burner of your mind, still operating in your unconscious but not dominating your thoughts. On the front burner, at the level of conscious awareness, the reason you engage should be simple: *just to have fun.* Just to share a few moments of pleasure, to have a conversation that's especially interesting or memorable.

That simple goal will pull you back to the importance of the here and now. With the exception of raising children, investing your energy in loving relationships is not at all like investing in the stock market, where you sacrifice now in hopes of big gains in

Strategies to Deepen Your Capacity to Engage

1. Remember: "Eighty percent of success is showing up."—Woody Allen

2. If you want to feel engaged, act engaged.

3. To deepen a moment of engagement, search for the emotion in the interaction.

4. Physical touch is the most potent form of engagement. Use it generously but wisely.

5. Express your liking and appreciation of your other clearly and frequently.

6. Remember that everyone needs and appreciates simple words of encouragement.

7. Be willing to change the context of your relationship.

8. Use the language of engagement.

9. Reveal your humanity. Perfect people set other people's teeth on edge.

the future. In love, the more you deprive yourself right now, the less you'll have right now *and* in the future.

So, blow your wad of engagement right now, for the sake of today. And do it again tomorrow . . . and the next day . . . and the next day. Because the real answer to *why* is simply to have a more enjoyable life. *Now.*

Strategy One: Remember: "Eighty percent of success is showing up."
—*Woody Allen*

To put it simply, you can't engage if you don't show up. Showing up doesn't mean having to be in the right place at the right time, for there is no one "right place." It really just means being some-place, *anyplace*, where engagement is possible. Engagement can't happen when you're parked in front of the television or when you're hunkered down at the computer or when you're sitting by yourself in the workplace cafeteria. It happens when you immerse yourself in the human world.

Remember, too, that it doesn't count as "showing up" if your mind is a million miles away. Show up with your fullest involve-ment with the interaction at hand. Show up with your ears, your eyes, your voice, your brain, and your heart. If you're going out on a date, *show up* with your fullest interest. If you're going to your kids' soccer game, *show up* with your team spirit. If you're lis-tening to your spouse talk about his or her lousy day at the office, *show up* with your sympathy and empathy.

If you're single and looking for someone to date, showing up is especially important—and challenging. During my single years, I sometimes showed up at events in hopes of meeting someone. That strategy took me to numerous cocktail parties where I hardly knew a soul and walked out to the parking lot alone. It took me to some community events where I wandered around watch-ing everyone else coupled up, obviously having a far better time than I. On one occasion it even took me to a weekend church retreat where the entertainment on Saturday night was sitting on a hard floor singing hymns trying to avoid the cockroaches that scurried by.

During that period I did meet some interesting men to date, but I never once met anyone by going to activities for the sake of meeting someone. I met people just by being out and about, which led to making new friends. My married friends occasionally set me up with single men they knew; that proved to be the best way to meet men, because they had been prescreened by people who knew us both. Although I really treasured my single women friends, I never met single men through them nor through activities we engaged in together. I met a few people at work and once or twice at the gym. I never tried a dating service or newspaper ads, though I know of several successful marriages that resulted from those sources.

I would recommend to any single person "in search of" that you show up at the places where you know you'll have a good time anyway. Build a solid circle of good friends, male and female, for they in turn have circles of friends. Live the fullest, richest, most fun life you can as a single person, but fashion it as a life in which you're "out there" in the world where love can find you.

Strategy Two: If you want to feel engaged, act engaged.
As you read this chapter, you may have had a nagging thought that you didn't quite want to admit—I know you did. You thought, "How in the world am I supposed to *show* interest if I don't *feel* interested?" Or, "What if I don't really give two hoots about someone I'm supposed to be trying to understand?"

Simple questions call for simple answers: *push yourself to act engaged long enough to allow something genuinely interesting to occur.*

Oprah, after all, surely doesn't feel engaged with every single guest on every single show, but she knows how to *act* engaged in a way that makes something interesting or exciting happen. Many times you will not feel in the mood to engage, or you may not feel there's anything going on worth engaging about. If you *act* engaged, however, you will often find yourself in interactions that do pique your genuine interest.

Why does acting engaged work? Because in acting engaged you naturally dig deeper into the interaction. Superficial conversation is inherently boring, after all. When you act engaged, you ask questions that push the conversation beyond the banalities of etiquette to find a more honest, and thus more interesting, point of contact.

Example: Yesterday I was waiting in the office of a local gas station to get my tires put on. A rather tired looking woman went to pay her bill and mentioned to the clerk that her husband was in a collar because he had broken his neck. In the midst of thinking about engagement, I decided to practice what I preached and said to her simply, "How awful."

"Yes," she said, "but that's not the worst of it. He slipped off a roof while he was working part-time so he doesn't get any workman's comp, and we don't have health insurance. Plus I just got laid off from my job, too." She turned and walked out the door.

In that brief moment, precipitated by my "acting" engaged, I experienced a small moment of connection. I was reminded of the extraordinary courage that working Americans show at times of extreme adversity. I reminded myself to buck up in dealing with whatever small problems I might have. I experienced deep gratitude for being in a relatively wonderful period of my life, with everyone in my family healthy and reasonably happy.

Let the behaviors of engagement become habitual. Act engaged whether you feel like it or not, and you will be startled how many more interesting and meaningful conversations and experiences you will just "happen" to have.

Strategy Three: To deepen a moment of engagement, search for the emotion in the interaction.

Emotions arise from an evolutionarily ancient part of your brain, the limbic system. The limbic system fires off a judgment about what's just happened: *Exciting! Awful! Funny! Enraging! Astounding!* Your limbic system tells you that something significant has happened, and in what way the event is significant.

As you engage, don't be afraid of your emotional response. Feel it, say it, show it. Communicate your own thoughts with emotion and respond to the emotions of others. Your active behavior enlivens a moment and makes it memorable. Your emotions reveal to your other how you are responding to the interchange and allow the two of you to develop a shared experience.

Further, search for the emotion in what your other is saying, and don't be fooled or distracted by "faux emotions." Often we protect ourselves from the depth of our feelings by covering one emotion with another; we make light of real disappointment or shrug off deeply painful experiences. We even do that with happy feelings, minimizing our success or downplaying moments of joy. Reflect what you know to be your other's true feelings, and don't join in the trivialization of authentic emotion.

Teenagers, boys and girls, are extraordinarily sensitive to each other's emotions and are amazingly skillful at sharing feelings with each other. That's why their cliques are so enduring; they experience life as a group, and the emotions of one become the emotions of all. While thankfully most of us mature beyond the stage of groupthink, we can nonetheless learn from their ability to enter into each other's world. Coach dumps on Jimmy, and Jimmy tells Sam. "Man, that sucks!" says Sam in eloquent sympathy. Mary gathers her girlfriends around her at the slumber party and describes how Joe finally got the nerve to put the moves on her. "That is so totally cool!" the other girls squeal in voyeuristic delight, and within twelve hours the whole school knows about it.

As adults, we lose that ability to really step into the world of each other's life. Maybe we're afraid of being overwhelmed or duped by others, or we learn to be judgmental of each other, to be skeptical of what we're hearing. Relearn the ability to *temporarily* suspend disbelief with your other—you can always later reprocess what you've heard if you're so inclined. And practice sensitivity to his or her nonverbal cues—the slump in his shoulders when he feels defeated, the spring in her step when she's excited—and reflect your awareness of those feelings in your words and behavior.

Strategy Four: Physical touch is the most potent form of engagement. Use it generously but wisely.
Everyone knows that sexual contact is an electrifying way to connect with a human being. But all forms of human touch are powerful, an instantaneous way of establishing connection. Touching someone at the right moment is an extremely effective way to connect—and touching at the wrong moment is terribly disturbing.

Touch conveys warmth and liking in the simplest and most primitive way, which is why shaking hands is so important at the first moment of a relationship. Testimony to how hardwired our need to touch is, think of how essential it is for babies to be handled frequently and lovingly; we all have that infant core within us. For that matter, all mammals connect with each other through touch. Just watch how dogs greet each other, how kittens curl up together, and how apes groom one another.

I recall a study performed years ago that showed that waitresses who lightly touch their patrons receive higher tips than those who don't. It's obviously possible to overdo touching, especially at work, but a light touch on the shoulder or elbow conveys kindness and acceptance.

When you're just beginning a relationship, nothing signals romantic possibility like subtle touch. You go to a football game with a group of friends and "happen" to sit next to someone attractive; the brush of your shoulders whispers a hint of things to come. You are working at your local bookstore and feel a special chemistry with a regular customer; the touch of your fingers as you give him his bag silently communicates your interest. You see someone on the rush-hour subway every so often who looks really interesting; a slight bump as you stand next to him on a crowded train is the opener for a conversation. And if those small interactions kindle a real flame of romance, nothing creates the blaze of sexual response like stroking an arm or touching an earlobe.

Nowhere is touch more important than in family life. Husbands and wives instinctively want to sleep together, for the love that's conveyed by an arm or a leg thrown over one's beloved in the early-morning hours is a conduit for a feeling of love that lasts for hours. Likewise, a hug given to a child that lasts only five or ten seconds carries him or her through the day. It may seem utterly obvious to you that touch is a potent form of engagement, but so many couples forget about the importance of the consistent, daily reapplication of this special glue.

Strategy Five: Express your liking and appreciation of your other clearly and frequently.

A friend of mine, Dick, had been lovingly married for several decades to a woman who was an identical twin. I asked him how they had met.

"Well," he said, "it was pretty funny. I had known my wife,

Paula, and her sister, Maggie, for many years. We had grown up in the same small town together. But we never dated until one summer I came home from college. My best friend and I wanted dates for Saturday night, and we thought of the twins. But they were so identical that we didn't know which one we should each ask, so we just flipped a coin. I got Paula and he got Maggie. I ended up marrying Paula and he married Maggie."

"That *is* so funny," I said. "You know, I've always wondered what it would be like to fall in love with an identical twin. Like, don't you find yourself in love with the twin as well? Don't you ever feel that attraction?"

"Oh, no," Dick responded. "I really like Maggie a lot, obviously. But I fell in love with Paula *because she fell in love with me*. It was really pretty simple."

Clearly half of falling in love with someone is based on admiration. But the other half, as Dick expressed, is that you fall in love with someone who falls in love with you. So, it's pretty simple. If you want to turn someone's *like* into *love*, show them that you love them. And remember to keep showing them. It's the most powerful form of seduction in the world.

Liking someone is also a reciprocal process, and you can easily and immediately increase you ability to convey liking by making it a practice to compliment others. A surprising majority of people have difficulty complimenting others readily. You may think highly of your other, but if you don't make your admiration explicit, he or she will never know how you feel.

One woman, Marian, had great difficulty establishing close relationships with others. A mutual acquaintance explained it this way: "You just never know where you stand with her. She never says anything bad to my face about me, but she's a generally negative person and never is very complimentary either. She's constantly bad-mouthing other people behind their back, so of course you know she's doing that to you, too. It makes everyone around her feel very uncomfortable." I would guess that Marian had no idea how her comments affected her relationships. She gained absolutely nothing by being critical, and it wouldn't have cost a nickel to pay a compliment.

This principle seems utterly obvious, doesn't it? Yet most people could easily and substantially improve their ability to convey liking and loving with just a little effort. So it's well worth observing the ways you do or don't show warmth to others, and commit yourself to improving in that area. It's something you can change *today*.

Strategy Six: Remember that everyone needs and appreciates simple words of encouragement.

Virtually all human beings strive toward something: to raise a child, to complete a job, to develop a talent or skill, to become a leader. In the midst of that struggle it's often easy to feel lost and adrift. At such moments, a word of encouragement is incredibly appreciated. Simple questions—"How's it going? What's your next step?"—convey your understanding of their efforts. Simple encouragement—"You're really making progress. All your hard work is paying off,"—is music to the ears of someone who wonders if it's all worthwhile.

Encouraging words are powerful because they reach your others at their point of need. You acknowledge their struggles and honor the importance of their goals. Your words connect you with them at that moment, pulling them forward.

Great coaches, leaders, and visionaries understand the importance of inspiration and encouragement. The simplest words are always the best. Think of Winston Churchill's speeches, which surely rank as among the most powerful words of encouragement ever uttered: "We will never surrender!" and "That was our finest hour!" The best-remembered and most inspirational of Churchill's utterances didn't offer complex concepts or use big words. They were simple, strong, powerful words of solidarity, support, and deep admiration of the people he led.

The best encouragement is honest. Refrain from giving dishonest praise, for your other will soon realize that your words are hollow and you will lose your credibility. A wise child psychiatrist once commented that the best way to ensure poor self-esteem in your children is to praise everything they do, for you are depriving them of the opportunity to build their self-esteem in a reality-based way. Don't tell your other that he looks wonderful when he doesn't, or that his work is brilliant if in fact it's mediocre. Find honest words that you and he or she can really believe. "You have a wonderful imagination" may be more honest than "You're a genius." "You have a way about you that really attracts people" may be more believable than "You're gorgeous."

If you really have nothing positive to say, you still have something invaluable to offer: constructive and useful advice, tactfully offered. If you have an employee or coworker who is not succeeding at work, explicit, concrete suggestions that will foster improvement are invaluable and deeply appreciated gifts. If your child's drawings are not on a par with his classmates, take the time to get a book about drawing and teach him the rules of perspective; he'll be thrilled. If your beloved's appearance is disappointing to both of you, make suggestions about the colors and styles you love to see him or her in. Then when you see real improvement, you can offer sincere compliments that will truly be appreciated.

Strategy Seven: Be willing to change the context of your relationship. Compartmentalizing your relationships limits the depth of engagement you can have. That's why, for instance, office parties are important; you need to see people outside their office cubicles to appreciate them as multifaceted human beings. It's also why something as simple as going to your child's class to help out or inviting his or her teacher over for a meal can be so meaningful. For a child there's a magic quality to seeing grown-ups out of context.

There's something particularly powerful and rather humorous about shifting to a context in which the rules of hierarchy are reversed, and you can use this principle to restructure your relationships. I recall one such moment, a day after the birth of my daughter. I was standing naked in my hospital room at the medical center, having just completed the sitz bath that I had been ordered to take. Without the warning of a knock, the door flew open and three medical students walked in. "We're student doctors," they said ponderously. "Delighted to meet you, gentlemen," I said, offering my hand with equal gravity. "I'm Dr. Austin, on the faculty in Psychiatry." My instant transformation from buck-naked-patient-with-no-right-to-privacy to faculty-who-might-someday-grade-them rendered my student doctors into blithering idiots, and they scuttled out of the room, thankfully never to return.

Try reversing roles with your child for a while; let your little girl be the mommy and you be the little girl. Or ask your student to teach you something that you honestly know little about. They'll be delighted.

There are infinite ways you can deepen your relationship by shifting context. Invite a workmate over for a meal. Ask your boss to play tennis with you. Take your child to work. Ask your spouse to help you with a project. Invite a friend to work at the homeless shelter with you. The shifts of context allow new facets of your relationship to develop, usually with delightful results.

Strategy Eight: Use the language of engagement.
The most golden form of communication is the simple question, and some questions connect you and your other particularly well.

"What was that like for you?" "How did you manage to get through that?" and "Where did you get the idea for that?" are examples of questions that invite your others to reflect on their experience and share it with you.

Likewise, simple comments often reveal empathy best. Dr. Leston Havens, in his book *Making Contact*, has written about the power of simple empathic comments. "Good God!" or "Oh my goodness!" are examples. My comment to the woman in the tire store "How awful!" borrows from Havens's way of using the simplest of utterances to convey understanding and concern.

There is also a body language of engagement. A big, toothy grin conveys connection in a way that a tight-lipped smile cannot. A big, hard bear hug expresses love, while a quick, stiff-armed embrace means your heart isn't really in it.

Greetings are particularly important. When someone you care about walks in the room or comes home for the evening, drop what you are doing to make him or her feel welcomed. Barely looking up from your task in acknowledgment reflects that you'd just as soon he or she was not there.

It used to be that if you said to someone, "How are you?" you'd hear back, "Fine." I recall occasional criticism about that boringly expectable reply. Now, however, I've noticed that when you ask how someone is, you will usually be greeted, "Busy. Really busy!" I once kept a secret tally of that response in my workplace and was struck that literally everybody gave the response "Busy." What was afoot? Was everyone really overwhelmed with that much work, or was there a new creed that not to be seen as "busy" would be like admitting you were a derelict?

Implicit in the word *busy* is the message "Don't expect too much engagement from me. I'm simply too occupied with other important matters to have time for that." I'd suggest, if you really want to have experiences of real engagement, delete the B-word from your conversation.

Strategy Nine: Reveal your humanity. Perfect people set other people's teeth on edge.
I have a secret to reveal: All people live troubled lives, at least at one time or another. No one escapes the messiness of human living.

I became convinced of this truism through practicing psychiatry for many years in Charleston, South Carolina. I truly love Charleston and its people, but I have to say that one of the quirks of Southerners is that they put great energy into conveying the impression that they live perfect lives. That gives rise to many wonderful aspects of the Southern culture: the emphasis on grace, charm, and hospitality; the solidarity of extended family; the beauty of homes and gardens; and the physical attractiveness and sense of style of Southerners. The problem, though, is that they actually start believing their own story, and when they find the same mental illness, substance abuse, and family dysfunction that every other group in the world has, they just don't know what to make of it. They get awfully embarrassed.

I've lived and worked in the South, the Mideast, and New England, and I've heard the secrets of every class, race, age, and culture living in those regions. No group has immunity from the most difficult human problems. Further, I have never spoken with a human being who has made it to middle age without experiencing a significant period of emotional pain or turmoil. No one makes it through life unscathed.

So why go to the bother of acting as if you have a perfect life? It's so boring. Either people will not believe you and will dislike you for being fake, or if some do believe you, they'll hate you for seeming smug. People don't love people because they're perfect but because they're human. No one is terribly interested in stories of others' good fortune, but they're deeply inspired by examples of humor, courage, perseverance, and the ability to learn from one's mistakes.

A Few Final Thoughts on Engagement: Defaults and Preferences

I recently bought a new computer, updated with the very latest operating system. As one who believes that a gig is a speaking engagement and a mega-Hertz is a humongous rental car, buying a new system was a little challenging.

One of the first steps in using my new computer was setting all the "preferences"—the default settings that control such things as font size, appearance of the background screen, and so forth. In fact, an infinite number of these "preferences" seem to determine every single tiny aspect of how the computer operates.

In other words, computers are really quite like your human mind. You, too, have established your own "preferences"—ways you routinely behave unless you consciously override your default mode. Setting your relationship preferences saves you the effort of having to make a million tiny decisions with each interaction.

Your preferences are what others experience as your basic personality.

They determine whether others want to engage with you.

Psychological preferences are unconsciously developed throughout your life. But they can be reset, and small changes may have an enormous impact on how your relationships feel to you and others. Here's a partial list of the enormous range of preferences that control the dynamics of how you engage. As you read through the lists, try checking off those that you have already established as your default mode; put an X in front of those you'd like to make automatic.

Tab 1: Greetings

❑ Smiles openly
❑ Shakes hands firmly
❑ Pauses to talk
❑ Greets family members at the door when they come in
❑ Remembers names of others
❑ Delivers full-body, two-arm hugs for those who are close
❑ Responds empathically to other's mood of the moment

Tab 2: Appearance

❑ Generally clean and neatly groomed
❑ Makes eye contact
❑ Shows self-respect through body maintenance
❑ Attends to dental hygiene and breath
❑ Avoids extremes in appearance that may be off-putting to others

Tab 3: Conversation

❑ Conveys genuine interest in other
❑ Avoids excessive criticism of those not present
❑ Communicates compassion and respect for those present and not present
❑ Is sensitive to painful issues
❑ Shares own feelings honestly
❑ Does not monopolize the conversation
❑ Remembers past conversations
❑ Listens nonjudgmentally
❑ Responds with appropriate emotion
❑ Sensitive to other's need to end conversation

Tab 4: Humor

- ❑ Laughs readily at other's humor
- ❑ Looks for humor in trying situations
- ❑ Quick to share a humorous insight
- ❑ Able to laugh at oneself
- ❑ Capable of having a great belly laugh

Tab 5: Sexual interaction

- ❑ Keeps body attractive for lover
- ❑ Willing to be spontaneously affectionate
- ❑ Doesn't flirt inappropriately
- ❑ Doesn't make lover jealous of others
- ❑ Willing to initiate sex
- ❑ Willing to allow other to initiate sex
- ❑ Willing to be experimental

Tab 6: Sensitivity to others

- ❑ Observes boundaries of propriety
- ❑ Aware of cultural sensibilities
- ❑ Respectful of age and station
- ❑ Aware of individual sensibilities
- ❑ Avoids overfamiliarity
- ❑ Does not divulge own personal issues in an inappropriate context
- ❑ Respects other's time constraints
- ❑ Responds to other's perceived mood state

Tab 7: Meeting new people

- ❑ Makes eye contact with strangers
- ❑ Speaks to strangers

❑ Shares humor with strangers
❑ Introduces self to strangers when appropriate
❑ Respects other's wishes to limit the interaction

Tab 8: Good-byes

❑ Communicates appreciation of the conversation
❑ Makes physical contact when saying good-bye, if appropriate
❑ Walks friends and family members to the door

As you deepen your ability to engage, your relationship life will expand significantly in both quality and quantity. You'll find yourself learning more about people you meet than you ever dreamed possible. That learning will help you decide which of your many acquaintances you wish to draw especially close to you. Consciously guiding the development of your relationships is the next step in getting the life you want. You do that by applying the ability to be empathic in evaluating the "fit" between you and others.

CHAPTER THREE

Evaluate the Choices
You Make for Love

I LOVE STROLLING through neighborhoods to enjoy other peoples' gardens and am often inspired to introduce new plants in my own garden. Several years ago I became enchanted by the roses I saw in a Charleston garden. I bought six bushes home from the nursery, planted them, and waited for a little bit of heaven to bloom in my own backyard.

Heaven lasted just ten days. Miracles of nature I had indeed, but in the form of battalions of Japanese beetles and aphids, which swarmed up the stalks and devoured the roses. And then there was the mold, spotting the leaves like a fungal Black Plague.

I went back to the nursery for a consultation. Not to worry, they said. If I sprayed my roses daily for a while, then every other day thereafter, then twice a week after that, my problem would come under control. They even showed me a pesticide tank I could strap on my back that would make my daily counterassaults easier.

Spray my roses *daily?* I can't even floss my teeth every day, much less suit up like a ghostbuster for a daily attack on marauding life-forms. I left the nursery empty-handed.

My roses never really died, but they looked increasingly scruffy.

An occasional forlorn blossom tried to survive, as if mournfully reminding me of all they could be if only I would do my part. As in human relationships, I had three choices: I could really take care of them; I could pull them out and plant something else; or I could let them limp along. Unwilling to face my mistake, I let them scraggle along for a few years before replacing them.

Your Human Garden

You live in a human garden, composed of all the people with whom you interact. You make acquaintances, and some of those develop into enduring friendships. You gather those friends around you to share the highs and lows of daily life. You may find someone to share a special love. And you may at times find a few unsavory characters in your life, people who choke off vital nutrients you need for your own growth. All of those relationships define the emotional landscape of your life.

As you increasingly practice the first Essential, *engagement*, you'll have a thought process just like mine during my neighborhood strolls. The more you reach out, the more new people will come into your life. You will find your own psychological world enriched by the people you meet. Soon you will want to bring some of those new people into your life. To be your friends, or maybe lovers. To make them your own.

But not everyone you meet will thrive in the conditions of friendship you're able to offer. Some people, wonderful though they may be, may not be right for you. Or perhaps they could thrive if you could only tend them well enough. But you may not have the time, the energy, or the desire to offer enough attention.

Plants from the nursery have little white tags on them that tell you what they need: *Water sparingly. Part sun. Fertilize lightly.* People don't come with tags, and yet each of us has a specific set of necessary conditions: *Avoid criticism. Compliment generously. Minimal stress. Needs plenty of space.*

You may not even be very clear yourself about what you need to grow and what will be toxic to your system. So you go by trial and error . . . and by wishful thinking, often underestimating your needs. Like my roses, you can survive in the beginning stages of a new relationship even if your conditions aren't met. And you can limp along for extended periods if your needs are sort-of-kind-of met. But you will never fully experience a wonderful love that endures if you ignore your basic requirements.

To tell you the truth, I could actually have predicted that the roses wouldn't do well in my garden. I should have found out just how much care they would really need *before* I bought them and had a heart-to-heart talk with myself about how much time I really wanted to invest in roses. But I didn't think it through for a simple reason: I wanted those roses so badly. I had wanted them for years. So my mind played a gentle little trick on me: I confused what I wished for with reality.

And so it is with people you bring into your life. You may love them and want them to love you so badly that your mind plays games with you. You ignore the clues they offer about what they will need from you. You're not realistic about how the conditions you can offer will affect them.

As if that weren't bad enough, it's only half of the problem. For just as you are taking your others into your garden, they are taking you into theirs. You are their rose and they are yours. You, too, have conditions you require for your survival. You, too, require care and feeding. Can your other provide those conditions? Can he or she offer the daily care you need?

The metaphor of the garden is only partly adequate in describing how you choose relationships. After all, "in my garden" or "not in my garden" is a simple, all-or-none, black-or-white choice—you make the choice once, and the plant is there to stay until it dies or you uproot it. Your human garden is much more fluid. There is a range of how close or how far people are to you, and that range shifts from activity to activity and from day to day.

The Importance of Choosing Well

How you "people" your world involves choices as small as whether you speak to the person in line at the grocery store and as large as saying yes to a proposal of marriage. And although choosing a mate is the single most important relationship choice you will make, you are challenged daily by potentially far-reaching decisions about whom to trust. You make decisions about who babysits your children, who repairs your car, and who fixes your toilet while you are out of the house. In your work life, you make decisions ranging from whom to work for, whom to hire, and whom to do business with. The success of your life—your ability to love deeply, to develop your ability to find joy, to work productively, and to sustain a sense of meaning—depends on your ability to be a good judge of character. When you're wrong in your choice of relationships, the consequences may be disastrous.

The human personality is extremely complex. Often you will see part of your other's personality and miss seeing other important portions. All of us hide much of our true selves from view. Some of the people you love the best may even have traits that blindside you. "He changed!" you'll say, when in fact those were parts of him or her that you refused to see.

Example: Jane was in love with Jim and decided that she was ready to get married: *Yo, Jim! Fish or cut bait!* Jim had mixed feelings about Jane. Yes, he loved her, and the last time they broke up he was really miserable. He certainly didn't want to go through *that* again, and he didn't think he'd find someone he liked better than Jane. But he really loved his freedom, and plenty of times he was glad to be away from Jane. Dating Jane suited him just fine.

But here was her ultimatum, signed, sealed, and delivered, even with a date looming when he would be sent back into exile. Jim was tortured. He asked her for some "space" for a few weeks— male code for wanting to sleep with someone else. But after a couple of dates with another woman, he missed Jane and one evening went over to her house and proposed. Jane was jubilant. He had committed!

But ambivalence doesn't end with a walk up the aisle. Yes, Jim said his vows. But once they settled down, he became moody and withdrawn. He began working longer hours and would often go out for a drink with workmates, leaving Jane alone. Saturday afternoons were often spent watching football games on television. He took up hunting and used vacation time to go off on excursions with his buddies. Jane actually found herself spending more time alone after they were married than before. In her words, "he changed completely."

Did he change? Not really. He had mixed feelings before the wedding, and mixed feelings afterward. But once married, he had no graceful way of not spending too much time with Jane. She had refused to understand the conditions he required.

As if the issue of mixed feelings weren't complicated enough, an additional problem makes it tough to choose wisely: all human beings reserve the right to change. As you and your mate are forced to adapt to new circumstances, you will both evolve. Will you both accept those changes over the years?

If you're starting to feel a bit overwhelmed by the challenge of making the right choices for your human garden, that's good. The biggest mistake you can make is overconfidence in your understanding of others. Set a goal of improving your ability to understand others with the assumption that you have lots to learn, that you *will always* have lots to learn, and that life is full of surprises. You never know another human completely, nor do your ever know yourself completely.

Finding a Soul Mate

Improving your insight into others will help all your relationships, but at no time is it more important than in choosing your mate. Unfortunately, though, it is never harder to think clearly than when you are falling in love. Romantic love is such a magical experience that the ancients described it as being shot by Cupid's arrow. You experience a powerful, maybe even desperate, wish to connect with your *enamorado*. But the more engaged your heart feels, the more disengaged your rational mind becomes.

What people call chemistry is really the result of an unconscious process of sorting through countless encounters to find the right mate. And how do you decide who that person will be? During childhood and adolescence, you begin to put together a mental scrapbook filled with bits and pieces of others whom you love and admire—male and female. From that scrapbook you begin to build a collage of the traits your ideal lover should have. Male or female? Older or younger than you? Your race, or another? You decide what core traits are essential, and what "bonus" traits are attractive, but less critical. An image of your ideal lover emerges, though it evolves over the years. The image is shaped by subsequent in-love experiences: if you are badly burned in a relationship, you may go out of your way to avoid certain traits that your last lover had. (*I'll never date another divorced parent!* Or: *No super-jocks for me!* Or: *Tortured artists need not apply!*) Parts of your image are conscious, but many elements are unconscious as well. In particular, parts that cause you to repeatedly make bad choices are often lodged deep in your unconscious mind, remote from rational scrutiny.

As you go through your life, you unconsciously compare your image with that of various people you meet. At times when your emotional need for a lover becomes particularly intense, you may even lower your standards and settle for a rough approximation of your ideal. Further, the lover who is "hard to get," just out of reach, is particularly exciting. You may be highly attracted to the mystery of your beloved, not realizing that the aloofness may simply mean that he or she is emotionally inaccessible for deep, intimate love.

One of the ways your unconscious orchestrates your choices is through your assumptions of what is "normal." Gia, for example, grew up in a highly argumentative family in which "normal" included dinnertime fights in which each parent hurled words and occasionally silverware to emphasize a point. Her father, an alcoholic, physically beat her mother on one occasion, which landed him in a rehab center. He eventually sobered up and the household became less violent, but Gia's assumptions of "what's normal" included a great deal of hostility and contention. In her dating relationships she was often argumentative, but for her, verbal fisticuffs were such an improvement over the physical altercations of her family that she thought these relationships were "normal." Her boyfriend William grew up in an emotionally constricted, unaffectionate household, and he was initially drawn to Gia's spontaneous emotional style. However, "normal" for him was minimal physical contact, and he thought they had a great relationship because they had sex once a week. Their polarized views of "what's normal" created real problems in their relationship over time.

Strolling down Memory Lane

If you're not currently in love, now is the perfect time to think through what you really want in your next relationship. You are in a period of rationality, in which you can think back about what didn't work in the past and evaluate what you really need in the future. You have the opportunity to resculpt your image of the perfect other, to lay the groundwork for your next love affair.

Think of the process of resculpting as reaching down deep into your unconscious and re-forming your image of a likely soul mate, like a sculptor forming a piece of clay. You're not trying to define a perfect person, but you are thinking through what a good match *for you* would be. You can't just do that through an intellectual process of analysis. You must really pull your emotions into the process, for your goal is to change your emotional responses. You will do that by taking a stroll down memory lane, remembering and reliving your past relationships, the good, the bad, and the ugly.

Set aside a special time to do this. If you like to write, sit down at the computer or grab a yellow legal pad and make notes of your thoughts. If not, find the setting in which you do your best thinking: in a warm bathtub with a candle lit, walking on the beach, or sitting on a park bench. Now, begin with your earliest memory of falling in love. Who was he or she? What happened in that relationship? How did it feel? What did you learn?

Now go on to the next relationship, and the one after that, and keep on going. What's important is emotional honesty, accessing the truth of what happened, what each of you did and didn't do, and how you felt during and after the relationship. If you have a good sense of humor, you may be able to amuse yourself by remembering your perceptions of your other before and after your affair:

DAVE, B.R. *(Before Relationship):* Oh! He has such a presence about him! He can just walk into a room and everyone stops to look at him!

DAVE, A.B. *(After Breakup):* What an arrogant, attention-seeking narcissist! He's such a grandstander, so vain and self-conscious.

Or:

KEVIN, B.R.: Oh! How romantic! A struggling writer! So committed to his work, to nurturing his genius.

KEVIN, A.B.: What a child! When is he going to grow up and get a real job?

Of course, if you really want to be honest, you may also wonder what your others have thought about *you* B.R. and A.B. Do you see any patterns?

The second part of your stroll is, what lessons can you learn from those experiences? What have you learned about yourself—your own needs, your problems in relationships, and what you are able to give another? What have the recurrent problems been? Is there a type of person you're always drawn to?

If you have trouble finding patterns in your relationships, dig deeper. If there really is no pattern, perhaps that's the problem: you fall in love too readily, too indiscriminately. You're letting lovers pick you, rather than you picking lovers.

As you identify a pattern in your relationship life, your first question is a simple one: *Is this pattern working?* Is this part of my behavior that I want to hold on to, or is it making me unhappy? What have I been blind to in the past that I need to open my eyes to? What warning signals of trouble must I become more sensitive to?

The second question is more challenging, for it requires a deeper level of self-honesty than you've perhaps dared to have before: *What are my core needs?* What are my long-term requirements that have to be met for me to stay engaged in a relationship?

It's hard to be honest because most of us underestimate our needs. We worry that our list is too long, that if we ask for too much, we will get nothing at all. So we shorten our list, compromising on really important issues, in an attempt to shoehorn ourselves into a relationship. But it's indeed like that pair of shoes that you loved so much that you ignored the wee bit of discomfort you felt in the shoe store—over the long term the fit really does matter a whole, whole lot. Points of friction don't go away, they just grow more painful.

Once in a relationship, it ought to be easy enough for you and your lover to tell one another what your true needs are, but it's not. You fear that if you talk about "the real thing," you will be too open and vulnerable. You fear rejection, and that would be unbearably painful. So both of you hide your true needs beneath a mantle of pseudo-issues, then become frustrated and feel misunderstood. Your challenge as a couple is to accept each person's needs as legitimate and important, and to be honest with each other if the relationship can't meet those needs.

I once ended a relationship in an unusually honest way. My friend and I had dated each other for several years. Though we were fond of each other, the fit wasn't quite right. One evening he said to me, "Linda, what are you really looking for in a man?"

"Someone who is warm and affectionate. Someone who loves books and music. Someone who enjoys long conversations."

"Well, that ain't me," he said without the least bit of defensiveness.

"And what are you looking for?"

"Someone who is sweet and happy all the time."

"Well, that ain't me," I said sadly but honestly. So we decided to part as friends. I suspect that one of the reasons we parted amicably was that we were able to acknowledge a simple truth, the same truth that is at the core of every breakup: we didn't love each other enough to say really mean things to each other.

Had we been yet more honest, our lists would have been much longer and more painful to discuss. He obviously needed more than just sweetness and happiness, or else I could have just loaned him my dog Zoey. (I wish I'd thought to say that at the time.) And I needed more than my three items, but they were simply the easiest ones to say at the moment. The older you get, the longer your list may become, for we all become increasingly differentiated in our likes and dislikes, and hopefully more honest with ourselves as well.

It's hardest of all to be honest about core needs that are so unusual that you fear you will never find someone who will meet them. As a psychiatrist, one of my core needs has always been "someone who is deeply interested in the life of the mind." That need alone sharply reduced my chances for finding a mate. If you're like most people, you, too, probably have unusual core needs. Some examples I've heard are:

"Someone who does not want to have children."

"Someone who can love my four children from my first marriage."

"Someone who shares my passion for wilderness exploration."

"Someone who does not want to live with me."

"Someone who can accept my mental illness."

"Someone who will convert to my religion."

Be honest about your core needs. The more clearly you can delineate those needs, the more easily you can identify your soul mate—and not be distracted by someone who simply is not.

Empathic Understanding

If you believe that I'm suggesting you take a cold, hard look at anyone you're considering falling in love with, you're right—and wrong. I do want you to take a hard look, but not necessarily a cold look. You're not evaluating the fit between you and your other to be judgmental, but to spare both of you unnecessary misery. Any potential "coldness" of your thoughts can be softened by your empathy for your other. Empathy is not the same as sympathy. Your goal is not to feel sorry for your other, but to accurately understand his needs from his point of view.

Empathy requires development of a *shared understanding* of your other. Empathy is not a onetime event, but an ongoing process that unfolds and deepens as the relationship builds. Your other reveals a bit of himself, and you openly acknowledge your understanding of that piece. Your understanding encourages him to reveal a bit more.

What I have described is only half of the process of developing a shared understanding of your "goodness of fit." The other half is allowing your other to be empathic toward you. That requires you to do something scary: *reveal yourself*. You want your other to be as empathic toward you as you are toward him or her, and that requires your allowing yourself to be really known.

Early on, it's easy to reveal the best parts of yourself, for the "in love" experience produces a euphoric high that makes you feel more joyful, sensitive, loving, and ennobled than at any other time—your In-Love Personality, as my friend Dr. Linda Godleski puts it. The real challenge, though, is to take the risk to reveal what she refers to as your True Colors, the real you that emerges after the psychotic denial phase of infatuation has worn off. You have to do that to allow your other to make a decision about whether the relationship is right from his or her side. Better now than later.

When your relationship is in the early gestational phase, there's a powerful wish to save your embryonic love at any cost. You try to hide the issues that will make your lover pull back from you. In the short run, it feels terribly painful to endure an early miscarriage of love. If that happens to you, console yourself with the recognition that that's just nature's way of sparing you the trauma of a long flawed relationship that was really never meant to be.

Empaths

The capacity for empathic understanding isn't simply an inborn trait. It actually is a skill you can build. In fact, all of us wax and wane throughout the day in empathy, for it's a lot of work and the truth is not always what we want. But the work is worth it, both in choosing your relationships and in keeping those relationships healthy.

Years ago, my twelve-year-old son and I went to a sci-fi movie in which certain characters were "empaths," capable of reading the minds of other people. Matt was absolutely intrigued with the idea of becoming an empath and asked how he could learn to read minds. "Just try it," I suggested. "I bet if you just listen very closely to what people say, watch their behavior, and pay attention to the little clues they give you, you can come pretty close to reading their minds."

For a few days he did just that. It was actually unnerving how well he could really read minds—mine and everyone else's. I began to feel I had no secrets my little swami couldn't guess. He eventually gave up his empathic behavior, not because he was unsuccessful but because it was tiring. Basketball was more fun.

When I meet people at parties and they learn I am a psychiatrist, if they are a little drunk, they will usually say, "Uh-oh, you must be reading my mind." In fact, I'm not, because it's takes a lot of effort! But in truth, the special ability that well-trained psychotherapists have to "read minds" is based on simply paying careful attention. Psychotherapy sessions are generally limited to fifty minutes because it is tiring to pay such close attention for a sustained period. But with simple practice, you also can "read minds"—if you have the energy for it!

The simple truth is that the vast majority of human beings can't help but reveal themselves. Most people, consciously or unconsciously, *yearn* to be known. Usually, that wish is conscious, and with little prodding most people will tell you their story: who they are, where they've come from, and something about their values, perceptions, and goals. Some people tell you about themselves quite directly, while for others there is a bit of disguise; it's up to you to learn to see through the disguise. As a relationship progresses, though, sometimes it becomes harder to know what is on your other's mind, particularly if he has begun to feel it's unsafe to share his thoughts openly with you. The more committed your relationship is, the more important it becomes for you to understand what's going on in your other's mind, for you have a lot invested. Here are some tips for trying to see through "the wall":

1. *Actions are more important than words.* Observe your other's behavior. Does he try to find ways to spend time with you, or do things seem to "come up" that are more important than you?

2. *Observe the themes of his conversation—they reveal what he really cares about.* Does he naturally seem to think and talk about you, your relationship, or your future plans together, or are his thoughts always dominated by work, hobbies, etc.?

3. *Observe his general emotional state.* Is he content, anxious, restless, optimistic, or pessimistic? What's triggering those feelings? Do you understand the depth of those emotions, and do they relate to your relationship?

4. *Take what he says at face value, particularly jokes.* That doesn't mean you don't laugh at his humor; beware of taking yourself too seriously. But if you hear recurrent patterns of jokes—for example, about having an affair, being attracted to younger women, or about your being fat or bossy—assume that these are issues on his mind. Pay attention!

5. *Observe body language.* Does he naturally sit with you, take your hand, or make eye contact?

6. *Put yourself in his shoes, and imagine how you would feel if you were living his life.* You may become aware of issues and concerns about which he may be in denial. Ask yourself how you would feel if he behaved the way you are behaving.

7. *Pay attention to Freudian slips.* Freud was right about slips of the tongue—they do reveal issues that are difficult to consciously acknowledge. (For instance, if he means to say "I like your sister's beer" and it comes out "I like your sister's rear," you may have a little problem.)

8. *Listen carefully if he tells you about his dreams.* The dominant emotional tone of his dreams communicates feelings with which he's struggling. Remember, though, that the particular details of dreams are symbolic; people he dreams about are used to represent themes he's thinking about, not the literal people themselves.

And, when all else fails . . .

   9. *Ask him what's on his mind.*

But if you do "resort" to #9, it's extremely important that you receive the information in a useful way—otherwise he'll just shut down the next time you ask him. That means you listen supportively, without becoming defensive. If he tells you something negative about your relationship, don't respond with a counterargument of your own; bring up your own issues at a different time. It's important for him to feel that something positive, not negative, comes from opening up to you, so if he mentions something in the relationship that you can work on, show him you've listened by making changes.

Reading the Mind of Someone You've Just Met

Of all of the time spent in a relationship, the very first moments of the first interaction can provide some of the most interesting insights into the character and needs of your other. Think of all the clues you may perceive within the first two minutes of conversation:

- Gender, approximate age, culture, and ethnicity
- Level of personal hygiene and attention to diet and exercise
- Degree of interest in personal attractiveness, ranging from extreme vanity to slovenliness
- Level of education, as evidenced by grammar, vocabulary, and content of conversation
- Place of origin, as evidenced by accent

- Degree of extroversion (speaks to you first, prolongs the conversations) versus introversion (the conversation dies unless you prolong it)

- Tendency to emphasize feelings and emotions versus the tendency to relate thoughts, ideas, and analysis (e.g., "I'm dying of the heat" versus "There's a low pressure system coming in")

- Need to impress others by dropping clues about accomplishments, education, wealth, etc.

- Ability to engage with others, as evidenced by interest and curiosity about you

- Emotional tone: happy, smiling, and humorous, versus flat, constricted, or even depressed

- Degree of reserve versus spontaneity

You can actually glean an enormous amount of important information almost immediately! Note that none of these first observations has anything whatever to do with whether your other is a good or bad human being. He may be an escaped murderer and nonetheless present himself as intelligent, extroverted, and highly interested in you. (Maybe a little too interested in you.) In fact, it's important *not* to confuse the superficial impressions of those first moments with an understanding of the other's true character. Your first impression is not about judging the other person; it's only about getting to know him or her a bit. It's the first step to becoming an empath!

The First Conversation: Manifest and Hidden Content

If you go beyond a casual brush-by and have a true conversation, you will learn much more. The first conversation is unlike any subsequent conversation, both in content and in form. It's a *positioning* conversation, with the goal of determining whether there is a reason to have a second conversation. If you do go on to a second conversation, the "real relationship" then begins.

In other words, that first conversation sets the stage for what may or may not follow. As such, it is extremely important, for you may not get another opportunity to connect. Your first goal, as a budding empath, is to try to understand as much as you can about what makes him or her tick, what's really important in his or her life. Your second goal is to let your other into your world by revealing something about what makes *you* tick, so the two of you together can decide whether you want that second conversation to occur. During any first conversation two questions are virtually always addressed by each person:

1. Do we live in the same world? Do we have anything in common at all, no matter how superficial, around which we can share a few words?

2. Is there any reason to think we might want to pursue a relationship?

The first question is superficial and concrete. Let's say you meet on an airport shuttle bus (as Jeb and I did), and the common ground is the trip you are taking: "Where are you headed?" or perhaps even "Can you believe that flight got in so late? I'm worried about missing my connection." None of those questions are factually important. (Why wouldn't he believe the flight was late? He was on it, too, wasn't he?!) But as the conversation proceeds, if the two of you are interested in each other, there will be exploration of more areas you may have in common. Perhaps you are going to the same meeting. Maybe you're both parents. Maybe you both have jobs that lead you to travel a lot.

But the real agenda of the conversation is the second question. You want to learn something special about your other to see if there is a basis for real connection. And you want to reveal something about yourself, to see if he or she can resonate with you.

The revelation of the "something special" almost always occurs via *disguised conversation*. When people try to relate something that is emotionally charged about themselves to you, they will speak in disguise, telling you a story about themselves that illustrates what they are getting at, rather than addressing the issue directly. What sounds like a factual story is really something of a parable. And that's where the "mind reading" comes in, because it's up to you to translate their parable into useful information—information that will ultimately allow you to decide if you want to draw this person closer into your world.

What is wonderful about parables is that so many levels of meaning are conveyed at once. Under the guise of telling you a story that happened "there and then," your other is trying, albeit unconsciously, to convey important information about "here and now"—your potential relationship. And once you've cracked the code—that is, looked for the relevance of the story to your budding relationship—your powers as an empath expand enormously.

So now let's put *you* on a shuttle bus on the tarmac of your local airport and practice translating disguised conversation into useful information. In the first conversation we'll pretend "You" are a woman who is generally available for a relationship. In the second conversation, "You" will be a man who is similarly available.

Conversation One

YOU: Can you believe how late that flight was?

HE: I know. I'm really worried that I'll miss my presentation. I knew my secretary shouldn't have put me on that flight, but I just couldn't get out of town any earlier.

TRANSLATION: *I'm a professional or businessman. I do important work, important enough that I travel out of town to make presentations. I also rate having a secretary, who makes my travel arrangements. And in case you didn't get that my work is important, my workday was so jam-packed that I had to risk being late for this out-of-town meeting.*

In one brief exchange you have learned quite a bit about your other. You've learned, for instance, that he is probably successful in his line of work. But you've also noticed that he seems to need to impress you. You've heard him blame his tardiness on his secretary. You've also learned that he probably overcommits his time, and you might wonder if his absorption in work limits his emotional involvement in his relationships.

Switch scenarios now:

Conversation Two

YOU: Can you believe how late that flight was?

SHE: I know. I'm really worried about getting back so late. I have to pick my kids up at their dad's, and he always has such a fit when I'm late.

Again, a veritable mother lode of information! In approximately seven seconds, you have learned that this woman is the divorced mother of at least two children, probably a center of love for her. Her motive in expressing this nugget of information may have been to let you know that she's single and available. Along the way, she's told you that she has a contentious relationship with her ex-husband. But with the sleuth of the empath, you have also gotten a hint that she *may* have a problem with tardiness (is she passive aggressive?) despite that there are unfortunate and predictable consequences for this behavior.

If you were a woman looking for a new relationship, would you be interested in the gentleman of the first conversation? Possibly. Maybe he's appealing because the last schmo you dated couldn't even hold down a job, and maybe someone who seems involved in his profession seems pretty neat. But he is also telling you about his conditions. He needs to be seen as important. He has a hard time accepting responsibility for his decisions, so you would need to put up with his blaming behaviors. His work is important to him. Can you deal with those conditions?

If you were a man looking for a new relationship, would you get involved with the woman of the second conversation? Maybe, if other aspects of her persona were appealing to you—there's always the issue of physical attractiveness, and maybe you have a soft spot for a pretty face. But she also has some conditions, right? You'd have to deal with her children, with her anger at her ex, and with her tendency to be late. No one's perfect. Everyone has conditions, and remember, you have yours, too. But are hers conditions to which you can accommodate?

Using that first conversation to decide if you want a second conversation is a humble goal. Yet it is indeed impressive what an enormous amount of information you can gather about another person. In fact, a few million years of evolution have allowed your brain to develop astounding perceptiveness about other human beings. Part of that ability is quite conscious, available to you as you think about the other you've just met. But an even larger part of your empathic ability is wholly unconscious: your mind registers thousands of subtle clues about the other: body language, posture, muscle tone, voice quality, eye contact, body odors, and on and on. All of those tiny clues are integrated together by your unconscious mind, and a simple answer is delivered in the form of a feeling: you're attracted, repelled, or unresponsive.

How reliable are first impressions? Think back to every long-term relationship you've had that ended badly. Now remember your very first encounter with that person. Nine times out of ten, you will be able to recall in that very first meeting the glimmerings of behaviors that eventually killed the relationship.

But think on. You will probably also remember many wonderful aspects of that person that were *not* apparent to you in that first conversation. Maybe Mr. Very Important also is an extremely fun-loving, adventurous person, with a good heart and a generous spirit, even if he is a bit too full of himself at times. Maybe Ms. Cute-but-Frazzled Single Mother is an exceptionally bright, creative person with a wonderful ability to form loving relationships and share generously of herself. You don't know, for your first impression is only a small biopsy of the total. But . . . it's all you have to start with.

Learning More

Assuming you move on to conversation two, you begin to learn more about your other. In particular, you start to appreciate the ways in which your other is unique—the strengths, weaknesses, and idiosyncrasies that make him or her different.

Scientists exploring the human genome have discovered that 99 percent of human gene material is identical for all humans—not so surprising since we all have to create the same sorts of blood cells, liver enzymes, and toenail protein as each other. But that 1 percent really does make a difference.

Likewise, as humans our personalities are far more similar than they are different. We all are driven to eat and sleep, to have sexual and aggressive urges, to laugh when something's funny and to cry when we're disappointed. We all comport ourselves in roughly similar ways when doing simple tasks, such as filling up the gas tank, brushing our teeth, or standing in line at McDonald's. But again, that small percent of uniqueness makes all the difference, and *that's* what you need to pay attention to in empathic evaluation. That small percent both makes and breaks relationships. Pay special attention to the ways in which your other is really different from other people—his or her greatest strengths and weaknesses. In time you'll observe a simple truism:

Our greatest strengths and our greatest weaknesses are one and the same.

Best/worst traits are personality drives that seek expression with intense determination. They can't be turned off and on at will. The identical traits that make us lovable and admirable are also expressed in ways that drive others around us just plain nuts.

In the early phases of the relationship, best/worst traits will be what you first fall in love with. You may be captivated by your lover's ability to love deeply, or you may be amazed by how much fun the two of you have together. You may really admire his or her ability to work or contribute, or you may be awed by the spirituality the relationship brings to your life. But you may be so overawed by that one strong trait that you may not realize that eventually it may cause other problems in your relationship.

Examples:

Jean's greatest strength was her extraordinary capacity to love deeply. She was enormously sensitive to the needs of others and felt deeply when those she loved suffered or struggled in any way. Her husband, Rob, fell in love with her kind heart and sympathetic, caring manner. Once they had children, however, he became frustrated because the needs of the children always came first. She was so sympathetic to their feelings that she would not leave them with a baby-sitter for an evening, much less a weekend. Even dinnertime was dominated by her attention to the children, and Rob felt increasingly remote from her and the family. His ability to have fun, to really enjoy his relationship with Jean, became extremely limited.

Isabel fell in love with Miguel because of his fun-loving, extroverted personality. Relatively introverted herself, she was drawn to his wonderful ability to engage with her, to draw her out, to expose her to new people and places. They married, and Miguel became a college football coach. He was a terrific coach because of his ability to engage with players, other coaches, university administrators . . . and fans . . . and potential donors . . . and students who needed help. Once the sports season started, she rarely saw more than the back of Miguel's head from the bleachers.

Jean's loving absorption was wonderful when it was directed at Rob; he found it not so wonderful when it was consumed by the children. Miguel's extroversion and sense of fun was wonderful when he focused it on Isabel; it was not so wonderful when it seemed to be focused toward everyone but Isabel. It was those traits that their respective mates fell in love with. The hard part was foreseeing, through evaluation, how those traits would play out in the long run within a marriage.

Hard, but not impossible. If you think of the greatest strengths of your other and then apply them to a situation you know will occur, your ability to predict potential problems will actually be quite good. You may love your lover because of his great intelligence and his capacity for self-discipline; but will you be happy with a spouse who works long hours or will you feel resentful and neglected? You may get a real kick out of your lover's fun-loving ways and nonmaterialistic approach to life. But are you truly willing to become the primary breadwinner of the home? You may enjoy your lover's quiet, calm personality. But if that also means that he will be passive in his interactions with others, will you remain tolerant and accepting? If the answer is yes, feel free to proceed with the relationship.

It is said that love is blind. The real problem is more that love is an emotion of the present. The *heart* has no sense of the future, of changing conditions and pressures, or of shifting relationship dynamics. But the *mind* can appreciate those possibilities, and you are wise to spend as much time rationally evaluating your choices as you spend energy immersed in the "in love" experience.

Fundamentals of Compatibility

Eight critical issues determine whether you and your lover will be true soul mates. The more you and your mate are compatible in these areas, the better your relationship will be. Any of these *can* be ignored during the early part of dating, and the tsunami of infatuation may sweep you into marriage. Over many years in marriage, however, lack of compatibility around these issues causes huge problems.

They spell the word E-V-A-L-U-A-T-E:

> E: Enjoyment
> V: Values
> A: Accessibility
> L: Love
> U: Understanding
> A: Attitudes
> T: Temperament
> E: Environment

E: Enjoyment: Do You Simply Like Being Together?

Enjoyment comes first in the list of compatibilities because it's a no-brainer—or at least, it ought to be! There's no point in being in a relationship with your other if it just doesn't feel good, especially in the earliest phases. Contrary to what we sometimes hear, great relationships really *aren't* a lot of teeth-gnashing, hair-pulling work. There aren't a lot of fights, struggle, and angst—as one of my long-married friends said, it's pretty smooth sailing. If you marry your lover, life itself will deliver plenty of struggles of its own—in the form of kids' problems, parent problems, money problems, health problems, and on and on. Those external problems will create enough challenges for your relationship without your creating additional ones yourselves. If you do argue a lot while you're simply dating, don't rush into a commitment.

Enjoyment should also take the form of bona fide *fun* at all stages of your relationship. It's easy enough to have a blast in those first months when you're both planning great dates. But over the years, fun too often takes a backseat to other demands of daily living. Nonetheless, if you and your mate have a shared sense of what's enjoyable and make those activities a priority, your relationship will retain its vitality.

Don't be afraid to ask for fun as a part of your relationship; we all need it throughout our lives, but too often it begins to slip away from our daily lives. Children know all about play, laughter, and joking. They live and breathe for fun, and wise parents understand that to get a child to do something, simply make it into a game. But then something happens. We begin to grow, and our parents start to discipline us. We go to school and learn that fun is experienced in little packets called recess. The teen years are often a struggle to express the childhood drive for fun and to resist the adult world's command to get serious. By adulthood, most of us get the message.

We start working more and more hours in the day, days in the week, and weeks in the year. We forget how to play.

For some people, the de-fun-ifying of life becomes so extreme that they hardly know how to have fun at all. Some such people have an *obsessive-compulsive personality*. They are rigid, perfectionistic, and tend to be emotionally cold and aloof. They become slaves to work and responsibility, forgetting how to be happy. Because of this, their ability to love may be compromised.

Not only do overly compulsive people forget how to have fun, but they begin to avoid having strong emotions of any sort, and their mental life is dominated by thought and analysis, rather than feelings. They are often good people, upright, proper, and dignified in every way; but they're not much fun. You may love your other because of his or her many ennobling qualities or because of the stability he or she brings to your life. But remember that without the ability to play together, the sparkle just won't be there. Pick someone you really enjoy being with—unless you just don't care much about fun, either.

A third level of enjoyment is the development of a shared sense of humor about the nuttiness of everyday life. Example: I had two dear friends whom I'll call Marty and Maida, his wife. They had the most incredible ability to sabotage any chances for financial prosperity they might have. Their calamities were notorious and much discussed by their friends, all of whom agreed that competence in anything of practical importance was not Marty and Maida's strong suit. When they bought their first home, they were overjoyed by its low price—until they learned they were living next to a toxic-waste dump. At another point, Maida decided they must invest in sterling-silver flatware. She waited years until sterling was at its peak price and bought a large collection. She then packed it in Pampers and put it in a plastic garbage bag, hoping to deceive potential robbers. It was such a clever disguise that Marty threw out the bag one day with the trash. On a third occasion, Marty parked the car at the top of a hill, but forgot to put the car in park. It rolled backward down the hill and landed in a neighbor's family room. Marty and Maida's daily life was enough to drive any normal couple to divorce court.

But their sense of humor was their saving grace. After the distress of an event had had time to heal, they would describe their latest misadventure in the most droll and witty way. Their friends adored them, and they adored each other—because they had so much fun together, even at the worst moments.

If you and your mate don't share a strong sense of humor, don't despair. Work on it! A sense of humor can be developed—it just takes a little effort. Remember that comedy is only tragedy plus time, and pause to find the insanity—and the joy—in daily life.

V: Values: What Is Important to You in Life?

For all of human history, societies have ordained that people should marry others of the same religion for the sake of preserving that faith. Times have changed, but there nonetheless remains wisdom in seeking someone with whom you share a sense of common values and meaning. That may require you to distinguish your formal religious affiliation from your true sense of meaning, for the two are not identical.

Rachel and Chris fell in love and married over the strenuous objections of their parents, for Rachel came from a devoutly Jewish family and Chris from an equally devout Catholic family. Neither converted, and they agreed to expose their children to both religions as they grew up and to encourage them to eventually make a choice. Despite the marked difference in their formal religions, though, their sense of meaning in daily life was actually quite similar. Both worked with children, Chris as a high school coach and Rachel as a dance teacher. They derived enormous personal meaning from the feeling of encouraging the development of the next generation. Both became involved in the Special Olympics and loved working with handicapped children. Both loved their family life and enjoyed activities with their kids. In fact they resonated with each other deeply in their shared sense of meaning, and it became a pillar that sustained their relationship.

The challenge of determining shared values is to distinguish authentic values from pseudo-values. The test of authenticity is whether one's stated values are reflected in how an individual invests his or her time, money, and energy. To get a more realistic assessment of your true values, ask, compared to a hypothetical "average" person, *how do I spend my time? Where do I invest my energy? How do I like to spend my money?* The same questions can be asked of a potential mate. It's easy enough for you and your other to *say* what your values are. The real issue is whether those values actually guide your choices and behavior.

You may gain insight into the true values of a potential lover by considering his or her work history and capacity to contribute to others. "Work" is not limited to paid compensation, for there are many ways to make a contribution to your community. But whether paid or unpaid, the way a person chooses—or chooses not—to contribute tells you so much about their character, including:

- Concern for the welfare of others: Has your other shown a sense of responsibility and interest for anyone outside his or her own family?

- Personal discipline: Has your other sustained a program of self-development (such as through education) or a commitment to a project that reflects an ability to tolerate the frustration of struggle and occasional setback?

- Respect for others: Has your other been a team player and shown respect and concern for coworkers?

- Work ethic: Do you and your other share a common work ethic—or lack thereof, if such is the case?

Vince, a forty-two-year-old advertising executive, is an example of how work history conveys rich information about a person's psychological life. Vince was an exceptionally bright and creative man and had achieved considerable success in his field. He had come through the ranks of advertising and was noted for a large array of talents that were useful in every aspect of his field. He had started in graphic design and was a talented artist. He had then moved into developing ad campaigns, for he was creative in developing slogans and strategies. From there he had become involved in the business aspects of advertising and successfully negotiated highly lucrative deals.

Yet, for all his talent, Vince had not really reached levels in his work of which he was truly capable. His work history was checkered; he would work for a firm for two or three years, then have a falling-out with his boss. On two occasions he had tried to start his own firm, but in each instance had run into conflicts with partners.

Vince had an explanation for the conflicts: "They're jealous. They know I'm talented, and they're threatened. My last boss was afraid I might try to get his job, so he found a way to get rid of me."

Clang, clang, clang! The alarms should sound in your mind if you hear your other blame repeated failures on the jealousy of others. An occasional failure, maybe. But when all conflicts are explained as due to jealousy, other dynamics are at play.

If asked, Vince might have said that his values included honesty, hard work, teamwork, and creativity. In fact, Vince really valued such unlofty ideals as making money, getting the credit, looking good, making a big splash, and outcompeting his bosses.

Anytime you hear repeated failures based on a single explanation, listen carefully. Your other is communicating to you much about his own unconscious dynamics that lead him to repetitive interpersonal problems. He is telling you about how he routinely interprets other's motives. The motives he ascribes to others actually arise within his mind and reflect his own values.

Obviously, all of us who work in groups have occasional conflicts with others. It really is possible to be victimized or misjudged or sabotaged. What's important to listen for, however, are repetitive patterns . . . because you can then predict that that history will be repeated with you.

A core part of values are reflected in your other's moral compass—his or her conscience. Conscience has several aspects: accountability for consequences; the ability to take responsibility and follow through; sensitivity to the needs and rights of others; and honesty even when it displeases others. Because your conscience determines how you negotiate with others, a well-developed conscience is a must for a healthy relationship. Most people have a working conscience in at least some aspects of life. But the real question is whether the conscience of your other has large gaps, like a chunk of Swiss cheese with gaping holes.

Most commonly, a poorly formed conscience results in chronic dishonesty. No one is perfectly honest all of the time; even the most honest people commit deceptions dozens of times a day, such as complimenting a friend who is fishing for a compliment or saying "No problem!" when you've truly been inconvenienced. Additionally, at times of extreme desperation many ethical people will omit telling the whole truth if the stakes are important enough. But if you observe that the deceptions of your other go beyond either a light greasing of the wheels of social intercourse or can't be explained by the direness of the circumstances, you can fairly predict that one day your other will turn his dishonesty on you.

Jerry learned the hard way that even relatively innocent lies can be harbingers of significant problems. His new girlfriend, Suellen, was a pleasant, attractive woman. Early on, though, he observed her capacity to shade the truth. On one occasion they canceled a dinner engagement with friends because they were exhausted. Rather than simply tell the truth, Jerry heard Suellen concoct an elaborate excuse about her mother being suddenly ill and needing her attention.

But the impact of Suellen's deceitfulness didn't become obvious for several months. Jerry became aware of small fibs, even at times when the truth would have served her better; she told him she didn't want to go to a movie because she didn't like scary films, when in fact she simply wanted to go to a different movie. But Jerry knew that the problem was more serious when a friend mentioned that he had seen Suellen at a restaurant on an evening when she had told Jerry she had to stay late at work.

For Suellen, dishonesty had become a way of warding off all potential unpleasantness. What should have alarmed Jerry after the first instance of lying was the facility with which she told a fib when simply saying "We're just too worn-out to be very good company tonight" would have been so easy. But dishonesty is an extremely slippery slope. Lying is such an easily available lubricant for the friction of daily living that it can become a way of life. Jerry was fortunate in that he ended the relationship with Suellen before making a lifelong commitment.

A: Accessibility: How Available Is Your Other for Real Emotional Connection?

Accessibility occurs at two levels: physical and emotional.

Physical accessibility is easy to evaluate. Is your boyfriend by your side for the important times in life? Does your girlfriend return calls when she says she will? Does your husband work such long hours that you never see him except when he's asleep? Is your wife always on the phone with her girlfriends or so absorbed by the children that she never has time for you? It's hard to have a great relationship if you don't have much time together. The most simple and obvious rule of thumb is that if your other really wants to spend time with you, he or she will find a way to do it.

Emotional accessibility is more subtle but even more important than physical accessibility. Are you and your other able to share your inner worlds? Do you talk about the really big issues? For that matter, do you enjoy talking about the funny, quirky events that happen in a day? Are there many topics that are off limits, or are you able to roam freely around a wide variety of subjects?

Emotional accessibility is conveyed both in conversation as well as in the nonverbals. Step back and observe what you talk about—and what you never talk about. Do you enjoy discussing the same things? If you bring up something that's really important to you, is he genuinely interested or does he change the subject? If you have a problem, do you have the ability to talk it through, or does your interaction deteriorate into anger or withdrawal?

Observe also the way the two of you communicate nonverbally. If you observe the other struggling with something—whether it's looking for a lost article, carrying a heavy load, or filling out your taxes—do you quickly step in to help?

L: *Love: Are the Two of You Similar in How You Experience and Express Love?*

A core need in choosing your mate is whether the two of you are similar in your desire and capacity to really love. In the beginning of the book, I commented that the foundation of love is loyalty, and people vary in their capacity to remain loyal. The characteristic of "good love" is the ability to genuinely care about the welfare of your other as much as you care about your own. Is that how you would describe your current relationship? Is that how you feel about your lover?

Even though a shared understanding of what it is to love is important, it may be tricky to gauge your beloved's capacity to love. In the infatuation stages of a relationship, most people love intensely and passionately—nature sees to that. The real question is what happens to love once the embers have cooled. There's even a brain physiology to that phenomenon—scientists have found that the infatuation stage lasts four years or less. What happens after that depends both on the relationship and on your individual capacities to love.

When you're first deciding whether your *enamorado* is right for you, take a hard look at the long-term relationships he or she has *with others*—and take a look at your own history. Are the patterns similar? If you have a lifelong pattern of wonderful, long-lasting friends, does he? If she has generally been a loner, have you? If you love being verbally and physically affectionate with others, does he?

If you find yourself thinking, well, okay, we have pursued our other relationships differently, but between *us* it's different—*stop!* It may be different now, but if your innate styles of giving and receiving love are mismatched, your relationship may not stay wonderful. With some effort at compromise, it may endure and may even be good. But it likely won't be *wonderful*, because you're missing the easy, reciprocal exchange of love and affection that leaves both of you satisfied.

It may seem utterly obvious to say that patterns of poor relationships are a warning flag that your other may not be the best person to become close to. But if you yourself are in the market for a new relationship, all your past relationships have failed as well, right? In fact, the only people who *are* available to you are those for whom every prior relationship has ended. So clearly, a history of past failed relationships can't be the sole criterion for evaluating the emotional health of your other. Most of us of have been in that position at some point in life.

By the same token, the assumption that anyone who has sustained a single long marriage is emotionally healthy is false as well. Some marriages are filled with hostility, coldness, rancor, or infidelity. In some marriages both parties maintain their emotional equilibrium by continually fantasizing about being with other people. Many couples are sustained not because of love and true partnership, but because of money issues, concern for children, religious issues, or fear of aloneness.

As you are getting to know your other, you will naturally want to predict what your future might be if you deepen your involvement. There is no clearer indication of future behavior than history. The challenge, however, is not to jump to conclusions—positive or negative—based on superficial observations, but to listen beneath the surface to hear how your other thinks about relationship issues—love, commitment, honesty, and the ability to tolerate frustration and disappointment.

Mark, sixty-two, came to see me because he was having difficulties in his second marriage, with Lorraine. His first wife, Mindy, had died three years earlier of breast cancer. Less than six months later, Mark married Lorraine, a woman he had known casually for many years. The relationship had quickly soured, for Lorraine became cold and critical of Mark; he suspected that she had married him only for his money. Mark was stuck. He was quite unhappy in his second marriage, but he just wasn't the divorcing kind. In addition, he was terrified of being alone.

Looking at Mark's situation on the surface, it is easy to be critical of his relationship instability. After all, didn't his remarriage so quickly after Mindy's death bespeak disloyalty to her and suggest that the first marriage had been poor? And what about marrying Lorraine so quickly and now being disappointed?

Yet, as I got to know Mark, I realized that he was in fact an emotionally stable man. He had had a wonderful marriage with Mindy and had nursed her lovingly through her long illness. When she died, he had been crazed with grief. He had never lived by himself, his grown children lived far away, and his circle of friends couldn't make up for the loneliness he felt. Just entering his home, half-expecting to turn a corner and see Mindy, made him weep in despair. He didn't marry Lorraine because he hadn't loved Mindy. He married because he had loved Mindy so much that his grief was just too much to bear alone.

As you are getting to know your other, take the time to listen and explore not just the surface content of what his or her past has been, but what the emotional meaning of that past was. When relationships have ended, has he felt victimized, or was he able to accept some responsibility for whatever difficulties arose? Have his relationships ended with some measure of respect and dignity, or has there been excessive chaos, anger, and contempt? Importantly, what has been your other's ability to sustain nonromantic friendships? Does he maintain a group of genuinely caring, loyal friends? The answers to those questions will give you a good idea of what your new relationship may have in store for you.

Compatibility in the physical expression of love—sex and affection—is as important as verbal communication, for when one person begins to feel withheld from, a marriage becomes ripe for infidelity. There is truth for many in the old joke that you can put a penny in a jar during the first year of marriage for every time you have sex, take a penny out each time for the rest of the marriage, and still have pennies left years later.

Because it's common for partners to gradually develop different levels of interest in sex and romance in ways that are hard to predict, it's important to at least share a commitment to communicate openly about those differences. Sexuality is an important part of the glue that holds a couple together. Without that glue, the relationship faces extra challenges over the years and decades.

Equally important as eroticism is physical affection. Individuals vary enormously in how much they enjoy physical touch. I suspect that a big part of that is innate, for parents of toddlers observe that from the get-go some children don't want to be held or hugged, while other tykes revel in physical affection. It's wonderful if you and your mate share a similar enjoyment of touch, whatever that level is. Otherwise, the less affectionate spouse experiences too much affection as being pawed, while the more affectionate one feels constantly rebuffed.

U: Understanding: Do You "Get" Each Other?

How easy it is for you to easily understand each other's emotions and reactions? Over time in your relationship you will probably be able to *predict* each other's responses, but that's different from being able to *understand* why your mate reacts as he or she does. Some examples:

Keith came to learn that Marie became extremely angry when she felt others were not loyal to or supportive of her. Keith, however, was a mild-mannered guy and couldn't really fathom the intensity of her feelings. Keith would often explain Marie's reactions by saying, "Well, that's just Marie," but he couldn't resonate with her intensity because he felt so differently. Marie married Keith when he was in graduate school. He was a disciplined student who worked long hours; Marie was fond of saying she hated school. Neither truly understood what motivated the other.

John and Mickie were parents of three children. Mickie was a devoted mother who was warm and affectionate with the children, while John was businesslike and sometimes stern with them. John thought Mickie overindulged the children, while Mickie couldn't understand why John didn't enjoy the children more.

Understanding is important as the basis for truly accepting your mate. Statements like "Well, that's just Marie" superficially convey acceptance; what they really mean is "I really can't explain why Marie is the way she is, but she's not going to change so I just have to live with it." Over the years, lack of understanding is a "little-*e* erosive" that chips away at a relationship. When your spouse behaves in a way that you simply can't understand, your admiration and respect begin to die.

If you're having trouble understanding your mate, try to get into his skin to try to see his life through his eyes. Ask him to explain how he's experienced a particular issue in the past, and what it means to him now. Be equally willing to share your own experiences. As you understand each other better, you will be less critical of each other's responses.

A: Attitudes: Do You Have a Shared Belief System about Roles, Responsibilities, and Activities of Daily Living?

"Attitudes" covers a broad range of issues in human living. It ranges from your attitudes about how family roles are determined to your views of political and social issues. Are you traditional or nonconformist? Open-minded or skeptical? Judgmental or forgiving? The issue is not whether you're a Democrat and he's a Republican, but how basic attitudes shape such family decisions as the importance of work, contribution to the family, responsibility, and equality in the home. Most importantly, do you have the same attitudes about your respective roles and responsibilities in family living?

For thousands of years of human history, the most powerful bond between a man and a woman was the work of creating and supporting a family together. Spouses were truly business partners, and their business was the survival of the family. The necessity of collaboration in order to contribute to the family, the village, and the church was part of the glue holding couples together. Roles were polarized, and both men and women were in danger of not fully appreciating or understanding the work of each other. Nonetheless, traditional marriages did have the advantage of clearly defined expectations of roles and responsibilities.

In modern two-wage-earner families, both partners may go in separate directions to work, returning to try to negotiate shared responsibilities in the home. Each person may or may not understand and respect the other's work, and the strain of dividing up household and child-rearing chores may be significant. It's important to have a bedrock of shared acceptance of what you expect from your respective family roles and a strong basis for communication over the years as those roles evolve. Talk about these issues with your mate, and make sure you have a clear understanding of your respective views.

T: Temperament: Are You Similar?

Temperament consists of all of the personality characteristics that are innate—that is, biologically determined. It covers a wide range of traits, including but not limited to:

Energy level

Novelty-seeking behavior

Predictability

Impulsivity

Mood regulation

Basic affect

Patterns of sleep-wake cycle

Irritability

Ability to self-soothe

You might think of all of these qualities as determining the *tone* of a personality. Just as a trombone and a guitar have different tones even when playing the same music, the fit between the temperaments of you and your other can create harmony or cacophony.

It's not at all necessary that you and your other have exactly the same temperaments—no two people do, for that matter. But pay attention to whether your temperaments are compatible, whether they seem to work well together. Being different by a notch or two on various characteristics often works well. Being diametrically opposite each other may require so much energy to negotiate the differences that you feel depleted and frustrated. It's fine, for instance, if your mate is a little moody and you're usually upbeat; but if the burden always falls to you to lift him out of his or her slump, you'll eventually feel overwhelmed. Likewise, if you're impulsive and your mate is predictable, you'll often feel constrained while your mate will resent feeling like your parent. Not good!

Because temperament is biologically driven, it's unlikely to change in the foreseeable future. If anything, the early stages of euphoric love often ameliorate problems in temperament. If you're concerned, think carefully.

E: Environment

Environment refers to all of the external conditions of a relationship that your lover brings with him—and all of the conditions that accompany you. It's on the list of fundamental compatibilities because environmental conditions can create severe conflicts for even the most loving couples. Together you and your other create a shared environment, with bits and pieces of each person's world. Can you live in the world you create together?

Examples of environment include:

Your families

Your friends

Your kids

Your ex-spouses, if they still make demands

Your financial status

A new community you move to because of the relationship

Effects of your respective class backgrounds

Required social interaction in each other's work world

Religious practices of your other that you observe

The impact of health needs

Demands of each other's work that intrude on the relationship

Cultural forces that affect the relationship

To understand more clearly what I mean by environment, imagine you went off to a Club Med and met a gorgeous stranger. Lolling on white sand beaches, scampering in and out of the waves, you fall madly, gloriously, deliriously in love. The week ends, the Club Med buses herd you out like so many cattle, and your dream week is over.

As luck would have it, you are suddenly transferred by your firm to the very same city as your lover! There you begin the relationship . . . in a very different environment. You have to spend time with his children from his first marriage. His mother lives in town, and Sunday dinners are spent with her. You want him to come to your business dinners, which render him semistuporous. He attends your church and is acutely uncomfortable. The two of you have very different incomes, which creates awkwardness.

It would be wonderful to think that the fundamental compatibilities E, V, A, L, U, A, and T were all that you had to think about. But that second E, *environment*, may present enormous problems that become make-it-or-break-it problems. Don't ignore those issues or shrug them off as minor problems. They're real, they're powerful, and they need to be considered when you're choosing a relationship.

Eight items to consider. It seems like a lot, right? It is, and that's why the vast majority of the other 4 billion humans are not candidates to be your soul mate. Yet out of that 4 billion, many really are great candidates. The challenge is getting out there where you're likely to meet at least one of them. And being patient until he or she comes along.

The Do's of Finding a New Romance

People stumble into "the right one" in three basic ways. The first and most common is simply by being busy with life, out and about where they are likely to meet people.

The second is by meeting people through friends. This, I think, is one of the best ways, for you have the advantage of a bit of pre-screening, helpful if you have friends with good taste.

The third way is through a dating service, computer chat rooms, or newspaper ads. The advantage of these routes is that your other has already identified himself as someone who's interested in a relationship. The disadvantage, of course, is that you may not be able to do much of a background check, potentially a major issue with computer contacts. *Caveat emptor!*

All of these strategies work, and if you're serious about finding love, I'd recommend that you consider all three. Remember that the bigger the net you fling, the more little fishies are likely to find their way to it. You then have the task of figuring out which one is a keeper. Following are some suggestions to guide that process.

Strategies for Finding a Soul Mate

1. Ask *all* your friends to be on the lookout for potential blind dates. Ask their spouses and beaux to help you look as well. Let your work associates know you're interested in meeting someone, and express your appreciation if they mention someone. Your friends will be able to screen out inappropriate candidates.

2. If you have met someone through the Internet, meet him or her in a safe, public place the first few times— for lunch, at a sports event, or at a community gather-

ing place. And don't let your on-line relationship progress too far before meeting your other lest you invest a lot of time and energy in someone who turns out to be a myth. If you begin to develop strong feelings for your on-line friend, remind yourself that you're falling in love with your fantasy of that person—and vice versa. Internet romances are terribly seductive because of the power of your imagination. There's something addictive about never knowing when a message will pop up in your in-box, and that excitement adds to the thrill of it all.

3. If you are using a dating service, investigate it thoroughly. Ask them what sorts of clients they have the most success with—age, socioeconomic status, etc. Find out what "guarantees" they offer before you plunk down your hard-earned money. Think carefully about what you're really looking for, and communicate you wishes as clearly as possible. Be careful about what you ask for, for you may well get it!

4. Pick out two or preferably three friends who truly love you and ask their opinion about the suitability of prospective swains. One friend alone may have his or her own motives for disliking your prospect, but if three friends all have their doubts, pay attention! Swear on a stack of Bibles that you will not be angry if they tell you the unvarnished truth, and that you will *not* pass on their comments to your *enamorado*. It's a sacred trust, so don't break it—they've risked a lot by being honest with you. Remember that your own ability to be objective is close to nil and you really need good advice about the most important decision of your life.

5. Your long-term comfort level will be best if you choose someone from "your village"—i.e., someone who comes from a similar value system, educational level, and traditions. Choosing someone exotic is exciting for at least a year or two but over time creates extra need for negotiation and compromise. Consider reestablishing contact with someone who was a platonic friend from your past; with the passage of time, you may well see each other with new eyes.

6. Ask questions. Especially in the early stages of dating, you may feel reluctant to ask questions about previous relationships. Don't be. You are entrusting your other with your emotional and physical safety, and you are making a substantial investment of your time, energy, and heart in the relationship.

7. Observe not only history, but trends of behavior over time. If your significant other has had difficulty with depression, is it getting better or worse? If he has had problems with alcohol, has he maintained sobriety for several years? If not, wait several years before deciding whether to marry. Marriage is a lifelong commitment, and it's worth the wait to be sure you're making the right decision.

8. Enter into his world. Meet his family, his friends, and his work associates. Observe him when he's under stress, when he's having fun, and when he's talking to his mother. Get as much information about your other as you possibly can before you make a commitment. If you see behaviors that concern you, don't be too quick to excuse them away. Remember that they may one day be directed at you.

9. Choose someone you can talk to as easily as you can talk to your best same-sex friend. Don't be seduced by your lover's air of mystery or by a sense that he or she is just a little out of reach. Probably you're observing that he or she is emotionally inaccessible, and that will only get worse during a long-term relationship.

10. Observe discrepancies between statements and actual behavior. If your other professes commitment but repeatedly disappoints you in small or large ways, pay attention. Assume that *what you see is what you get*. Yes, it is always possible for people to change, but don't bank on it. After all, your other has already had an entire lifetime to make the changes you are hoping to see!

11. It's a bad sign if you and your lover have multiple breakups while dating. You are breaking up for good reasons that should not be minimized or ignored. Truly compatible people who are deeply in love don't break up.

12. Don't rush the relationship. Pace your dates. Allow the initiation of phone calls and dates to alternate between you. Let the initial craze of infatuation subside before making lifelong decisions.

13. Keep your finger on the pulse of your emotional responses to your other. If you begin to feel uncomfortable, don't ignore it; important truths about yourself, your other, or the relationship may be contained within that early warning.

Finding a wonderful other is critically important—but of course it's only the first step of a relationship. As important as who your other is, who *you* are in your relationships is even more important. After all, you can always dump your other—but you can't dump yourself.

So it's time to turn your attention to an even more challenging question:

What is your capacity to truly love another human being?

CHAPTER FOUR

Expand Your Safety Zone

FOR THE FIRST FIFTEEN YEARS or so of my practice as a psychiatrist, most of my patients were women suffering from mood and anxiety problems. Some were single, perhaps newly divorced, and were depressed because they experienced great loneliness and isolation. They worried that life was passing them by, often feeling like hungry children with their noses pressed up against the window, watching a banquet to which they were not invited. They feared they would always be alone.

They faced a very real problem. The transition from married to single is extremely difficult for most people. The temptation to find an instant exit from the feeling of isolation can be overwhelming, and often these women were tempted to jump into new relationships that were even more inappropriate than their marriages had been. Could they tolerate aloneness long enough to wait for someone who was really right for them, regardless of how long that took?

A second group of women in my practice were depressed because their relationships were miserable. I would usually recommend couples therapy for them. In general, if the marriage was fundamentally sound and the couple still loved each other, therapy was extremely helpful. But for some, the marriage was just too far gone. Within the relationship one or both of the individuals had a significant fear of connecting too deeply with the other. That fear may have stemmed from childhood experiences or may have resulted from repeated wounds within the marriage. *If I open myself up, will I be ignored again? Will I be rejected if I reveal my vulnerabilities? Will I sacrifice too much if I give more to my mate? Will I be suffocated if I became more intimate?* For those husbands and wives, the fear of connection with each other was overwhelming. Some of those women stayed in their marriage not because they loved their husband but because they did not believe that real connection was possible with anyone. "I know what's out there," they'd say. A deep cynicism pervaded their feelings about love, and marriage was primarily a business relationship.

After fifteen years as a practicing psychiatrist, I had developed a good grasp of female psychology. It was the early nineties, heyday of the John Gray *Men Are from Mars, Women Are from Venus* philosophy. I realized that I knew so much less about male psychology than female, and I wanted to learn more about this alter species of humans that was giving women such fits. I looked forward to studying fascinating differences between men and women, and I also hoped I would learn more about women by seeing them through the eyes of men.

So I began to treat as many men in psychotherapy as I could and saw quite a few in once- or twice-weekly psychotherapy that usually lasted several years. I enjoyed treating them every bit as much as I did my women patients. What really amazed me was that, by golly, John Gray was wrong. Men aren't from Mars and women are not from Venus. We're all earthlings, and we all struggle with most of the same core issues, though the superficial window dressing of those issues looked different.

The men, those beasts that women shrilly accused of being unwilling to commit, actually seemed extremely interested in long-term, stable relationships. If anything, they seemed even more scared of isolation than women, maybe because women were more confident of having same-sex friends. In fact, when the men found themselves single, they seemed even more willing to grab the first warm, breathing person they found, not because they lacked "standards" but because they couldn't stand being alone.

And just like my female patients, men also had fears of connection. Just as women feared being dominated by a man, the men feared being dominated by a woman. Just as the women often disguised their true feelings beneath a mantle of faux feminine wiles, the men often hid out behind their masculine bravado. So while the camouflage appeared different, the fundamental issues were very much the same. If I were to show you transcripts of the men's and women's psychotherapy sessions with identifying gender clues disguised, you would rarely have been able to tell which gender was which.

This is not to say that both genders don't blame their relationship problems on "fundamental" sex differences. The men would heave enormous sighs, roll their eyes heavenward, and moan, "I guess women are just like that." Women would likewise heave huge sighs, moan, and say, "I know men are just like that."

What I learned is a simple truth: People are "just like that." Men and women are scared of the same issues of human living, although they may use different personality mechanisms to deal with their conflicts. Unhappy men often retreat to alcohol while women more often retreat to food. Unhappy men withdraw from women into solitude and work, while unhappy women barricade themselves against men with a cadre of women friends.

Your Safety Zone

Whether you're male or female, the twin anxieties—isolation and connection—have enormous impact on your ability to find the love you want. So utterly unconscious are those fears that you are usually unaware of how they shape your behavior. But think, for a moment, of how they influence people who are close to you. You probably know someone who is so uncomfortable with closeness that she holes herself up in her home, joyless night after night. You may know someone else who is unable to commit to a relationship because she is unwilling to give up control of aspects of her life. Another friend may feel that life has no meaning if she is not in a love relationship. As humans, we are both scared of aloneness and uncomfortable with too much closeness. We bounce back and forth between those two psychological forces, thus losing the serenity of simple love.

If your mind were laid out neatly in zones, you would be able to identify specific anxiety zones. The zone of connection anxiety would include all of the perceptions and interactions with others that make you uncomfortable. If you lack self-confidence, for instance, it might include all people who make you feel insecure. If you're a control freak, it might include everyone who disrupts your sense of organization. If you have difficulty with intimacy, it might be anyone who challenges you to come closer. It might be wonderful to have no connection anxiety, but we *all* define certain types of people and interactions as uncomfortable.

A second area would be your zone of isolation anxiety. The size of that zone varies enormously. For some people the slightest whiff of rejection triggers massive amounts of abandonment fear; their isolation anxiety zone is as big as the sky. At the opposite extreme, true loners have *relatively* little isolation anxiety, although I've never heard of anyone living by choice in total solitude.

In between those two zones is your *safety zone*, a mental state in which you feel comfortable and secure. Optimal mental health could be defined as a large safety zone, allowing you freedom of movement between loving relationships and times of solitude. For some people, though, the safety zone becomes so small that anxiety becomes overwhelming.

Years ago, I evaluated a woman named Penny who came to see me for therapy ostensibly because of post-traumatic stress disorder. A decade before, she had been menaced by a coworker and had become extremely anxious and depressed. Although she had been treated for years by another psychiatrist for PTSD, I was unconvinced that this one incident could account for the subsequent years of symptoms. At the time I saw her, she had not worked for many years. She avoided all contact with men and would not go into a room alone with any man other than her husband. But she also had great difficulty being alone and controlled her husband by making him accompany her to any new places. She was clearly depressed and anxious, but reacted to tiny doses of medication with exaggerated and bizarre side effects. She responded to the mildest comments from me with storms of emotion and became indignant and offended if I made the least suggestion that her symptoms had taken on a life of their own. Her safety zone was minute, and she seemed to want to keep it so. I did not feel she was motivated to do any true therapeutic work with me, and at my suggestion we ended the therapy.

Penny is an extreme case, but inability to create a safety zone with plenty of freedom of movement is a common problem leading to a variety of everyday behaviors. Often this takes the form of overemphasizing another part of your life as a safe haven where you can avoid your fears. You may become a workaholic, escaping to work to avoid closeness. You may overinvest in your children to avoid interacting with your husband. You may use your religion

not in a life-affirming way, but to avoid the challenges of relationships in the here and now. Or you may use "quick fixes" through compulsions such as drugs or alcohol; social anxiety is a major cause of alcoholism.

As you ping-pong back and forth between your fears, your life becomes destabilized and then constricted. You're unhappy as a single person, for you hate the loneliness. You then leap into another disappointing relationship, then begin to make unreasonable demands on your other. This happened to Rhoda, whose dread of both aloneness and intimacy was profound.

Rhoda, an attractive woman who worked as a real estate agent, came to see me for psychotherapy because she was miserable. Everything in her life had come easily to her. Love also came easily to her—too easily. Over and over she destroyed relationships by "loving" two men at once.

"I just don't know what to do. I feel crazed, I can't sleep at night, I can hardly even look at food. All I do is think about Mike 1 and how I can get him back."

"Mike 1?" I asked. "Is there a Mike 2, or Mike 3?"

"Thank God there's just a Mike 2. And he's everything you'd ever want in a boyfriend—it's just that I can't get Mike 1 out of my mind.

"Mike 1 and I lived together for a couple of years. We were like true soul mates. We had incredible sex. You wouldn't believe it, it was like something out of a movie. We had great conversations. He was a really deep thinker and he read a lot. We could talk about anything—it was like he could read my mind, and I could read his. But we'd get in fights. He was sort of a hippie and never really settled down at a job. I could kick myself now that we'd have fights about it. I made plenty of money, so what was the big deal? But he'd get on my case, too, about why I was so work-driven. I'd move out for a few months, and sometimes I'd start

dating someone else, but I'd always go back to him. Finally I got a great job offer in another state, and we decided I'd go there and try it for a while. Then a few months after I left, he found another woman, Darla. I know he doesn't love Darla—in fact he tells me that and says that he still loves me. He still writes me just amazing letters—next time I'll bring you one so you can see.

"So then I met Mike 2. He's everything that Mike 1 is not. He has a steady job. He's really even-tempered, always pleasant. And he really loves me. I've even told him about Mike 1, and he's very understanding, he says he'll be patient with me. To tell you the truth, he's even much better looking than Mike 1. And he wants someday to have kids, which Mike 1 would never have done. So why can't I fall in love with Mike 2?"

For several months Rhoda agonized over the dilemma of Mike 1 versus 2, engaging in dizzying discussions of their relative merits, their deficits, the ups and downs of her passion for the charms of Mike 1 and her aloofness toward the hapless Mike 2. Then, out of the blue, Mike 1 called her to say he had broken up with Darla, desperately missed Rhoda, and was relocating to be with her. Rhoda quickly gave Mike 2 the old heave-ho and went back to Mike 1, dropping out of therapy for a period. After a year, however, she was back:

"I just can't believe this. I moved in with Mike 1. Within a few days, I knew I'd made a huge mistake. He's so temperamental, and it really irritates me that he's financially dependent on me. What really kills me, though, is that I just heard that Mike 2 is getting married. I can't believe I was so stupid. I called Mike 2 and I could tell he's still interested in me—he agreed to have lunch with me."

What in the world was going on? Why was the grass always greener—or the other Mike always more enticing? Rhoda was terrified of aloneness and couldn't stand being without a man— she always had one, if not two, in her life. But she also couldn't

stand being truly intimate with a man and would use fantasies of her last relationship to push away from her current love. She had virtually no anxiety-free zone, but jumped back and forth between her fears of closeness and fears of connection like a tribal dancer on hot coals.

If you are holding yourself back from love, it may be that you, too, feel claustrophobic in the tiny safety zone between isolation and connection you have created. Finding and sustaining love requires you to push back the boundaries of anxiety that keep you from deep engagement with others. Is it possible to become less anxious? Absolutely. To begin that process, it's necessary to understand how anxiety works.

Just What Is Unconscious Anxiety?

The anxiety that is stirred up by relationships is related to an ancient emotion, fear. Just as when you're afraid, you may feel anxiety as a tingly, tense vigilance that sets you on edge and makes you uncomfortable in your own skin. Like our animal cousins, humans are fearful of threats like poisonous snakes or scary animals. But our evolution allowed us to feel a similar fear when confronted with menacing or unknown people on the one hand, and the threat of aloneness on the other.

Having created anxiety as an interpersonal warning signal, the human mind now faced a second problem: the capacity to feel anxious and tense all of the time. Many people suffer from this condition; it's called generalized anxiety disorder. Most of us, however, can use anxiety as a warning signal without having to feel continually uptight. We keep most of our anxiety tucked away in the unconscious. We modify our behavior when interpersonal danger is near *without even realizing we are doing so.*

Unconscious anxiety is so locked out of your awareness that it's hard to appreciate how profoundly it affects you. But think of it as similar to your fear of fire. You probably can't remember how you learned that fire was hot, or the first time your hand came too close to a flame. When you are now near a flame, you do not consciously think, "It's hot; I'd better not touch it." But unconsciously you are guided by that fear when you're close to a flame; you draw near, but not too near. Not until someone waves a candle in your face are you aware of danger.

Anxiety not only makes you avoid things, but it also shapes complex patterns of behavior, just as fear does. When you stand at the top of a stairwell, you don't think about the danger of falling. But as you take each step down, the dozens of muscles controlling your feet, ankles, thighs, body posture, and even the hand holding the stair rail are perfectly synchronized to keep you from stumbling. You learned those movements in early childhood and you perfected them through years of repetition—highly complex motor movements that keep you safe. Likewise, interpersonal anxiety has shaped your relationship behavior in thousands of tiny ways.

Think of anxiety as a small but powerful robot living in the deepest, darkest recesses of your mind, giving a "Go!" or "Halt!" command in response to every action you intend to make. That robot of yours keeps detailed files of all your past experiences, and it constantly refers back to them to figure out if your behavior is safe or not. It's always scanning the environment to make sure you end up neither isolated nor overwhelmed by others. The robot has no concept of helping you find rich, satisfying relationships— its only goal is emotional safety.

But it may also be holding you back from getting the love and the life you want.

Is There Room in Your Safety Zone for Your Other?

Anxiety has extraordinary power to define the emotional territory in which others feel relaxed with you. If your lover encroaches on your territory, you will behave in ways that will drive him or her away. You may become churlish and irritable or pick fights or become a control freak, causing him to pull up stakes and flee for dear life.

Worse yet, anxiety acts entirely in the moment, without regard to the long-range consequences of its directives. It may have such a powerful hold that it makes you sabotage your deepest desires. Paradoxically, *anxiety creates the very conditions it is trying to avoid.* Examples:

- Myrna's deepest dread was that she would never marry. She was so desperate to get married that she prematurely raised the issue with every man she dated and behaved in such a suffocating way that her boyfriends invariably bolted in terror.

- Paul's anxiety was that he would end up a financial failure like his father, whom his mother had berated throughout Paul's childhood. In his mind, wealth would be the ticket to love; he couldn't believe he could be loved for the goodness of his heart or the warmth of his personality. Paul chose to become a stockbroker, although he basically hated the intense stress of every day. When the market took a serious beating during a recession, he lost most of his wealth due to his investments in volatile stocks.

- Kelley's dread was that she would become fat; for her, the ticket to love from a man was a thin body. She repeatedly put herself on diets, but was so obsessed with food that she felt chronically irritable, starved, and deprived. She would then binge, which indeed caused her to become obese.

- Lee's greatest fear was of making a fool of himself in front of other people. He was a pianist and an accomplished musician. However, when it came time to perform, he was virtually disabled by anxiety: his hands trembled and sweated so much that he would stumble badly through his program, and he eventually gave up performance altogether.

These are somewhat dramatic examples, but they do illustrate the ways in which anxiety creates what it seeks to avoid. Perhaps you want so much to be liked that you try to impress people with your looks, wit, or accomplishments; they're irritated that you are more concerned with yourself than with them, and they back off. Perhaps you want so badly to be a good parent that you overprotect or overcontrol your child and end up with a rebellious kid. Perhaps you are so scared of being rejected that you try too hard to please others, and they find your submissiveness unpleasant.

The second paradox of anxiety is that *the more you try to avoid situations that make you anxious, the more anxious you become.* People with social anxiety, for example, may first become panicked while giving a speech. Next they worry about becoming panicky at social gatherings, so they go out only with close friends. They may then choose jobs that have limited social interactions, withdrawing even more. In extreme cases, they may even stop leaving the house much at all. Had they been able to resist succumbing to their original fears, they might have avoided the cascading series of fears. There is truth to the advice to "get back in the saddle."

For all that anxiety is such a powerful psychological force, here's the good news: you can lower you levels of unconscious anxiety and expand your safety zone *by doing the very thing that makes you anxious*. You can start in a small ways, with brief forays into new behaviors and responses. Every time you challenge yourself to stand up to your anxiety, your brain becomes less sensitive to its power. But before you can begin retraining your brain, you first have to understand just what is scaring you and how your unconscious mind is shaping your behavior.

The Terror of Isolation

The most powerful of the interpersonal anxieties, I believe, is the terror of isolation.

Dread of isolation can take several forms. I'm not referring, though, to an inability to spend an evening or a weekend alone so long as you're in a relationship. The issue is whether you can tolerate periods of not having a primary source of love, the lover who loves you best—*psychological singleness*. Without the ability to tolerate singleness, you will be driven into some relationship, *any relationship*. Your dread of aloneness will cause you to act like the Fairy Queen in *A Midsummer Night's Dream*, falling in love with the first jackass you lay eyes on.

Fear of aloneness can become so marked that everything else in life becomes devalued. Many teenage girls, for instance, become pregnant for one reason: "I want to have someone to love me." Unwilling to commit themselves to the discipline of work or school, unable to find happiness in other relationships or personal development, having a child becomes the permanent "fix" to avoid having to be alone.

Take a breath now, and go one step beneath the surface of

everyday awareness to ask yourself what exactly about aloneness is so scary. For most people it is the belief that *you need someone to give you something you don't feel you can give yourself.* If you can learn to provide that something, you will become far more able to tolerate aloneness. As an added bonus, you will become a much easier person for others to love. All your relationships will become healthier.

Sometimes even the most confident-appearing people are ruled by fear of isolation, as was the case for my patient Dave. Fun, intelligent, and insightful, he seemingly had all the ingredients for a happy relationship. But like Rhoda, he worked his relationships like a relay race—the second one had to get going before the first one stopped. Dave never truly *chose* his relationships; it would be more accurate to say he *grabbed* them as they floated by, without really examining whether they were right for him. He couldn't bear remaining partnerless long enough to search for a really good match. I challenged him to understand why being alone was so scary.

"Well," he said thoughtfully, "the hardest time for me is in the evenings. That's when the stress of work gets to me. I just start feeling really edgy and tense. If I have a girlfriend to call or go out with, it makes it better."

Of course the company of a girlfriend would make it better in the short run; after all, talking to others is a great way to feel soothed and comforted. But because that was the *only* way Dave knew of to manage his feelings, he lacked the psychological freedom to choose aloneness. For all the appearance of the unfettered bachelor, he was actually quite leashed to his girlfriends, choke chain around his neck.

Further, Dave's need for his girlfriends to manage his emotions had an impact on the quality of his relationships. His various honeys had a variety of responses to this role. One encouraged Dave's neediness because she could then saddle him with her own emotional problems. Another found his neediness tiresome and fled the relationship. A third put herself in the role of his therapist and began to impose her solutions on his problems.

Had Dave been a less attractive man, he might not have had the option to jump from girlfriend to girlfriend, crossing the icy river of aloneness floe by floe. Perhaps he would have sought treatment earlier in life and used psychotherapy to explore the root of his tension. He might have learned, for instance, that at work he relived old wishes to impress his father, and his girlfriends were substitutes for his soothing mother. Perhaps he would have realized earlier that his work was too stressful and looked for a different job. Or maybe he would have found other ways to decompress at the end of the day. Any of these choices might have been healthier for Dave, whether or not he was in a relationship. He might have understood that his girlfriends couldn't really fill him up with security; as quickly as they poured comfort into him, it drained right out again.

Some people cling to bad relationships because they're afraid of having to regulate their own self-esteem. Donna, a midlife woman married to an alcoholic, bad-tempered salesman, described her choice this way: "My husband is a tough man to be married to, but the marriage gives me a place in society. To the outside world we look like a respectable family, and I have some financial security. If I left, I'd have to work, and I'd have the stigma of being a divorcée. I've always felt sorry for single women, and I hate the thought of people feeling pity for me." For Donna, merely being in a relationship made her feel better about herself, even if interacting with her husband actually battered her self-esteem.

Donna needed to deal with her self-esteem issues head-on, rather than hiding behind the screen of "Well, at least I'm married." She believed that the marriage gave her self-esteem, while, in fact, it was her poor self-esteem that led her to tolerate her husband's bad behavior. Had she been forced out of the marriage, she would have had the opportunity to find ways to improve her confidence. She would have had to find employment, and work is one of the best ways to boost self-confidence. She would have drawn on family and friends who would have been far more comforting than her husband. She might even have been able to give up the chronic resentment she felt in her marriage, opening herself up to a more peaceful life.

Donna voiced yet another reason underlying the fear of aloneness: "I don't want to grow old alone. I have diabetes, you know. The doctor says that if I would just lose weight and exercise, it would probably go away, but I just can't get the willpower to do it. I'm scared of all the complications of diabetes—like blindness and kidney problems. Who would take care of me if I got sick?"

I challenged her to examine that thought. In fact, if her husband was nasty to her when she was relatively young and attractive, why would he suddenly become kind and giving through the mere passage of time and the advent of old age? The odds were equally high that she would end up taking care of him rather than vice versa. If she disliked being with him when he was at least healthy enough to care for himself, why would she want to be his caretaker when he deteriorated into alcoholic dementia and cirrhosis?

Many people drive themselves into relationships out of fear of growing old alone. In fact, the real "fear behind the fear" is growing old and ill at all, and no relationship can prevent that. If your marriage has been empty during your young, healthy years, it will not transform itself into a source of comfort once you and your mate are old and infirm.

Distorted Behavior

Anxiety about aloneness distorts your perceptions and shapes your behavior in numerous ways. Some of the behaviors it produces are:

- *Panic or anxiety when alone:* The feeling of anxiety ranges from a low-level tension or restlessness to a full-blown panic attack. Much as a claustrophobic person feels terrified because there's "no way out" of a confined space, your anxiety comes from a feeling that there's no way out of your aloneness. You fear you will never find another love relationship, and life seems to stretch endlessly before you.

- *Extreme discomfort when not in a love relationship:* I have actually heard more men than women describe this feeling. It's sometimes expressed as a sense of being "incomplete" when single. Your discomfort leads you to hook up lest you become unhinged. Often this leads to rebound relationships.

- *Enduring hurtful relationships:* You put up with repeated disappointments and frustrations in your relationship, but keep thinking to yourself, "Well, it's better than being alone."

- *Revisiting the scene of the crime:* After you break off a relationship, you go back one or more times because you can't tolerate the lonely nights.

- *Passive or submissive relationships:* You are often quiet and subdued around your other. You worry about speaking up for yourself because you fear it will lead to an argument, and you can't stand the threat of your other's anger or coldness.

- *Clinging behavior with friends:* You're generally the one to initiate contact with friends, and more than one friendship has ended because you were suffocating. If you become aware that a friend hasn't been in touch with you, rather than let the friendship breathe, you demand to know why. You sometimes use guilt to manipulate friends into spending time with you.

- *Discomfort with eating or traveling alone:* You would never dream of going to a movie or restaurant by yourself. You worry that if someone saw you, they might feel sorry for you. On the other hand, you like being seen out with people, in part to let others know that you're in demand.

- *Difficulties spending a weekend alone:* You don't know how to enjoy the pleasure of your own company, to relish the peace and quiet at being alone with your thoughts. You may become depressed or anxious, and you fear having to manage difficult moods by yourself.

- *Unwillingness to live alone at some point in adult life:* The only way to avoid living alone at some point is if you marry young, continue living with your parents, or always have roommates. If you've avoided ever living alone, you've missed an important experience.

People who behave in these ways often see their isolation fear as a sign of weakness. Actually, it's the other way around. Because you have a core idea that you're not strong, you don't believe you can regulate your moods and tolerate uncomfortable feelings. You become afraid of your fear and search for ways to avoid the alone-ness that triggers it. Remember that an idea is simply an idea. It is less than air and only has the power you give it. You thought it up. You can unthink it, but you have to make a real effort to challenge that thought.

In fact, most people who have lived with others much or all of their life find the transition to singlehood extremely difficult, so don't be dismayed if you find yourself scared at times. It's a common, understandable fear to have, and one that you can overcome.

Three ways to go about healing your fear of isolation are by (1) *examining* your anxiety, (2) *extending* your reach gradually, and (3) *exploding* your fears by what I call shock therapy. You can try all three:

Examining your anxiety: If I were working with you in therapy about your fears, I would start with the question "Why are you afraid, and what exactly are you afraid of?" Maybe you're afraid of what aloneness means to you; it may carry implications that you're unloved and unworthy. Or maybe it feels as if your alone-ness will last forever, that you've been thrown out to orbit end-lessly in outer space. Maybe you're afraid of the moods and emotions you might have while alone. Ask yourself why aloneness feels so dangerous to you. Just putting it into words will help you contain the feelings it stirs up.

Think of yourself as having an inner reservoir in which uncom-fortable feelings—sadness, hurt, fear—are contained. Your goal is to increase the size of that reservoir. No one escapes pain in life, but we vary enormously in our ability to tolerate it. When anxiety takes hold, we become like small children screaming at the sight of a needle in the doctor's office; the fear is far greater than the ac-tual pain. If you can decrease your anxiety, your emotional pain will dramatically lessen. Even setting the goal of increasing your toleration of discomfort is an important step, for you are mastering the anxiety that exaggerates your reactions.

The second question I'd ask would be "Where does this fear come from?" Were you a child who was often left alone, and now your old fears of abandonment have been stirred up? Did you have an alcoholic parent who often left you alone to deal with scary situations? Did your mother make you feel that popularity was everything? Are you still stuck back in junior high school, feeling as if you'll never find a group who will accept you? Think back to your earliest memories of aloneness. Are you still feeling echoes of those old experiences? Remember the mantra *That was then, and this is now.*

The third question of examination is "What is this fear doing for you now?" In other words, why are you holding on to the fear? Is it because you would otherwise have to take real responsibility for managing your life? Is it scary to let go of the thought that Prince Charming will come and make all your problems go away? Do you enjoy having people around you worry about you and fear that, if you were strong, you might be forgotten?

These are the questions I explore with my therapy patients. They're questions you can explore yourself or may want to talk to friends about. I'd strongly recommend working with a skilled therapist if you have hit a roadblock and you're aware that your safety zone is small. If you're at a crisis point now, you may be at a point to do some real work on these issues.

A second way to work on your fears is by *extending your reach*. This is a concrete behavioral approach, for after you have gained insight the time comes when you actually have to change. Extension is a gradual approach to change. You keep pushing yourself just a little to do things that seem a little scary to you. Some things you can try doing alone are:

- Go to a movie.

- Take a beach walk.

- Join a health club.

- Take yourself out to a good restaurant.

- Go to a cocktail party.

- Join a service organization.

- Go to a concert.

- Take a class.

- Join a running club.

Start out by doing these things in the simplest way possible. Once you feel comfortable, take a second step: when you go to these places, practice talking to strangers. Your goal is to learn that you are able to have fun . . . alone. Your goal is to desensitize yourself to aloneness.

Another way to extend your capacity to enjoy singlehood is to learn to enjoy the pleasure of your own company by staying home . . . alone. Start with a day, then a weekend. Use the time just to think. Limit phone calls, limit television, and limit the computer. Practice just thinking your thoughts, observing your feelings and reflections. Feel the peace that comes from quietude. Indulge yourself in simple pleasures that require solitude: uninterrupted time with a good book. A quiet walk at sunset. An afternoon in the hammock listening to a great CD.

The third step is *exploding your fears* of aloneness by a major, dramatic experience. Nothing does that better than taking a trip by yourself, whether that trip is going camping by yourself in a state park near home or going to a foreign country by yourself.

I had an experience like that several years into my life as a single person. As one who had shared a bedroom with my sister, loved having college roommates, and married while still in college, I had more than my share of fear of aloneness when I first divorced. I explored the roots of my fear and disciplined myself to extend my reach by doing activities I had never before done alone. After several years, though, I had the opportunity to go to France by myself. I was scared, but I did it.

I had been to France before and loved the country. I speak shameless French, well enough to make French people think I'm conversant, but not well enough to understand what the hell they're saying when they actually talk back to me. Further, the French are bafflingly uncomprehending if one makes the tiniest error in pronunciation. Try slightly mispronouncing an address to a French cabbie—like ask to go to the famous store Chanel. You could easily end up in the Chunnel.

Nonetheless, I had the time of my life in Paris. I learned an invaluable lesson: when you travel by yourself, people are infinitely kinder and more outreaching than when you travel with others. Solitary travel is an entirely different experience from group travel and is a great adventure. One afternoon I talked to two little ladies at a café who were going to an off-the-beaten-track museum; they reminded me of Flora and Fauna in *Sleeping Beauty*. My awful French was matched by their awful English, and they swept me up along on their excursion. We spent the afternoon chattering away; I would laugh merrily at their jokes without having the remotest notion of what they were saying. Another night I struck up a conversation with an Italian pilot who comically tried to pick me up, despite a prominent wedding band on his finger; I toyed with him mercilessly and enjoyed every minute of it, asking endless questions about his wife and children. I talked to people standing in line at museums, and they would invite me to join them. It was an enormous step for me in learning to enjoy, really enjoy, my life as a single person.

There are a number of ways to explode your isolation anxieties. Volunteer to house-sit for your sister or friend. Go to a church meditation retreat. Move to a new community. Ask your boss to send you on a business trip. In time you'll see your isolation anxiety begin to melt.

The main reason to overcome your fear of isolation is simply to improve the quality of your life during times when you're not in a relationship. But you'll discover a wonderful side benefit. You'll be much more "fit" for finding a great relationship. Others will find you much more interesting. You won't cling to inappropriate relationships out of desperation. You won't smother your other if he chooses to withdraw from time to time. You'll feel your self-confidence improve, knowing that within you is the power to enjoy the simple pleasures of life. As you learn to enjoy the pleasure of your own company, others will, too.

The Opposite Danger: Connection

Most of us are aware of how scary and painful isolation is. It's harder to be aware of our anxieties about connection because they are often more subtle and more unconscious. Since you're at least motivated enough to improve your relationships that you've taken the time to read this book, you may feel that fear of connection is the furthest thing from your mind.

Beyond that, if you're a reasonably sociable person, maybe even extroverted, you may feel somewhat aggrieved at the thought that you may have connection anxieties. *What, me? Look at the wide circle of friends I have. Look at how loyal and committed I've been with my best friends through the years. Connection is my middle name!*

Yet all of us have connection fear in at least *some* corner of our relationships. Connection anxiety is not an all-or-none phenomenon. It's usually partial and episodic, appearing only in particular dynamics of your closest relationships. If you took the time to analyze the roots of your connection anxieties, you would observe their origins in past experiences of hurt or betrayal.

Not one of us has come through life unscathed. As children, we all experienced feeling small, vulnerable, and ignorant of the ways of the world. Children live in the hierarchical world of children, bestowing status and privileges on each other based on size, age, and savvy. Even the hardiest of us endured frustration and humiliation at the hands of each other. At times we were laughed at, excluded, or misunderstood—it goes with the territory of childhood. Sometimes we misperceived the motivations of others who may only have been doing their duty as loving parents or teachers. At other times we were challenged to perform tasks that were beyond our capabilities, experiencing the shame and humiliation of failure.

And those are only the *normal* experiences of childhood. Perhaps your own experiences of hurt went beyond "normal." If you grew up in an abusive household, or in a home where tragedy struck through illness or the death of someone you loved, your scars may go much deeper yet. If a parent had a mental illness or a substance abuse problem, your sense of emotional safety may have been drastically diminished. If you yourself were born with any sort of biologically based difficulty—ADHD, learning problems, mental health vulnerabilities, or an unusual physical appearance— you may have suffered severe feelings of rejection and shame, particularly if no one was there to help you through the tough times. If you were born in a financially disadvantaged home, or you were the victim of racism or ethnic prejudice, you may have developed extrasensitivity to feeling deprived, shut out, or put down. You may have learned and grown stronger through trauma, but you may also have developed toughness or cynicism that make it difficult to maintain closeness to others.

Even a life of privilege creates its own wounds. One young man, born into a wealthy family and fortunate enough to have been sent to an excellent private school, commented on his experience of growing up: "I don't think people understand what it's like to have people constantly telling you how lucky you are. You can feel their envy, and it doesn't feel good at all. Even in school, our teachers were always making comments about how we kids just didn't understand the real world. Some of them made it pretty clear that they saw us as stuck-up, but I think we were just trying to be kids. If I went to a party with the public school kids or played on a sports team across town, they'd make digs about my preppy haircut, or my rich dad. I have to go the extra mile to come across like a regular guy, and not to talk about big parts of my life that might make other people feel jealous. I get pretty tired of it. I don't make digs about their lifestyle, so why do they have to make comments about how I live?"

I came to appreciate how repeated small comments can whittle down self-esteem when I was on a medical school rotation with my friend Valerie. I liked Valerie but she seemed to have a chip on her shoulder. At four feet eleven inches she was obviously short and complained frequently about her height. I didn't understand the impact of her height until we worked together. Throughout the day, I heard a numerous tiny comments about Valerie's height from patients, doctors, and other students. "You don't look tall enough to be a doctor!" "We should get you a stool to stand on at the blackboard!" "Did you have trouble finding a white coat in your size?" No one comment was particularly cruel, but the frequency of the comments, all coming from different sources, chipped away at Val's self-esteem and made her self-conscious.

We all have wounds—you, me, and everyone else. There are

two ways to respond to a wound. You may develop scar tissue, and your toughness may look like strength, invulnerability, cynicism, or aloofness. Alternatively, without that toughness you may continue to have an open wound, extrasensitive to slights or tending to overinterpret the behavior of others. Either way, your ability to remain connected to your other will be diminished. If your wounds are relatively limited, your areas of connection anxiety will be small and not terribly damaging to your relationships. Large wounds, however, can create major problem areas in your relationships, and you must get to the heart of the matter to heal yourself or even to excise excessive scar tissue.

Talk openly with your other about your wounded places. Ask him or her for their love and patience as you work to improve your relationship. Be compassionate with yourself as you try to understand your own behavior; you didn't ask to be wounded, after all, even if now only you can heal your hurts. As humans, we learn from our past, but we can learn bad lessons as well as good.

If you've ever been badly betrayed in a love relationship, you may have become so mistrustful that you push loving people away from you. *I dare not care too much, or I will be rejected.* Your fear of rejection may be activated only in romantic love relationships, or it may become so generalized that you push all people away from you.

My patient Karen, the daughter of a mentally ill mother and an alcoholic father, had had a childhood of shame and dealt with her deep wounds by creating a zone of unapproachability around her. She described to me how uncomfortable she felt doing something as simple as attending her children's sports events:

"The parents there are really pretty snobby. They all know each other, and none of them ever talk to me. I hate how shallow they all are, like the only thing that matters is their status and who has just bought a new car or bigger house. I dread going to the games for that reason, so I always sit apart from them. Sometimes, if there's not much room, I'll even sit with the parents of the other team instead of our own team."

I'll reject them before they reject me. Karen was a human cactus, prickly spikes warning others to keep their distance, living apart in a desert of her own making. Karen's behavior exemplifies how anxiety creates what it seeks to avoid. Surely not *all* the parents of her kids' teammates were snobby, nor was it likely that they had hatched a unified plan to exclude Karen from conversation. More likely, she was seen as aloof and unfriendly, and when she sat with the other team's parents, she was probably seen as just plain weird. In fact, Karen lived her life making preemptive strikes. She slammed the door on others before they could slam her out.

Karen's behavior is unusual only in degree. Think of the times you have not offered an invitation to a new acquaintance because you were unsure whether your gesture would be welcomed; the times you have stayed out of a conversation due to lack of confidence; the times you didn't move over on the high school bleacher and invite a Karen to come sit with you.

These are concrete behaviors. More subtly, the fear of rejection may wrap around you like a shroud, muffling your voice and paralyzing your movements. Every time your fear of criticism blocks you from saying what's on your mind, you miss an opportunity to engage deeply with others. You push others away, holding them at arm's length, keeping the interaction in a safe place, constricting your terms of engagement. You block yourself from getting the love you yearn for.

One of the warmest and most interpersonally skilled men I've ever met described his personal philosophy in an interesting way: "I always assume that people will like me and that there is plenty to go around." Plenty of what? Karen needed to understand there was plenty of room on the gymnasium bleachers for one more parent and time in the day for one more conversation. Plenty of room for one more friend and for acceptance of her human faults and foibles. There was plenty of time for a belly laugh—or a good cry—over the moments of embarrassment, chagrin, conflict, outrage, and struggle that fill a human life.

If you anticipate rejection, you will be rejected. If you anticipate acceptance, you will be accepted. Changing your expectations requires taking a huge risk with your self-esteem. You remind yourself that no one was ever loved because he or she was perfect, but because he or she was human. So you draw a deep breath and reveal the nutty, flawed, humble side of yourself—the part of you that allows others to be human as well. With each risk you demonstrate your wish to engage. You enlarge your safety zone. You take a step toward love.

If feeling shy and self-conscious is holding you back from connecting with others, you can use behavioral strategies to change your behavior. You can try a number of techniques, but one of my favorites is *role reversal*. I learned this, actually, from an older woman, Hester, who had suffered for many years from shyness in social situations:

"For most of my life I've had problems with self-confidence. The way I finally got over my problem was kind of interesting. When I'd go into a situation—let's say a cocktail party—instead of thinking about myself, I'd look around the room for the person who looked the loneliest, the little wallflower standing off alone. Then I'd go over and talk to them, instead of waiting for someone else to talk to me. I'd have the loveliest conversations sometimes, and I got so I could usually have a pretty good time at those parties."

From a psychological perspective, what had Hester done? She had stepped out of her customary role as the shy one and had allowed herself to see someone else in that role. She had then reversed her shyness into the behavior of becoming kind, generous, and outreaching toward others. She veered off from her customary direction and stopped the pattern of circling back into anxiety and isolation.

Reversing your assumptions can lead you to experiment with very different ways of interacting with others, opening up continents of new experience for you. Let's imagine, for instance, that you're the opposite of Hester. You might have a great deal of social confidence. You assume that others are impressed by your looks or clothes or find your achievements remarkable. Think of the ways those assumptions would affect your behavior. You might unconsciously carry yourself in a way that others perceived as haughty. You might become a bit aloof, feeling that others aren't quite at your level. You might be tempted to dominate conversations, as if you assume that others are more interested in your life than their own.

So what would happen if you reversed those assumptions? What if you thought that rather than being impressed by your appearance, the first impression others had was that you were vain and shallow? What if you thought that rather than feeling beneath you, others felt mildly sorry for you because you seemed lonely and isolated? What if you assumed that rather than being impressed by your achievements, others found your self-absorption boring and pathetic?

Immediately your behavior would change. You might actually take less pains to create a great appearance. You would be more outreaching and friendly, and you would start to show more interest in others and more modesty about yourself. You would probably become a much more lovable human being. And much more attractive to others.

Fear of Loss of Freedom

A particular form of anxiety over closeness is fear of loss of freedom. While women often complain about men's difficulty in making a commitment, men worry about losing freedom in relationships. Remember that males and females have a different experience growing up, for both genders are typically raised primarily by mothers and educated by mostly female teachers. Many girls grow up thinking "Someday I'll be like my mom—powerful and controlling in the home." Many boys grow up thinking, "Someday I'll marry someone like my mom—powerful and controlling in the home." It's scary.

Jesse's pattern for twenty years had been to find pleasant, younger women to date; like most men, he believed he looked unusually youthful for his age. He would typically hang on to the relationship for two or three years, investing himself enough with the woman to encourage her to fall in love. Nonetheless, when the topic of The Big M—marriage—would arise, Jesse would become just a wee bit vague, offering just enough reassurance to make his girlfriends think he would eventually come around. When pushed to the wall, however, he would end the relationship. This pattern continued until he was in his midforties and had dated a woman for four years. Weary at the thought of yet another breakup, he finally agreed to marry. Once married, however, he immediately regretted his decision and became withdrawn and remote from his new wife.

Jesse's mother had died when he was three years old. A year later his father remarried a harsh, unloving woman whom Jesse perceived to favor her own children. Growing up, he left home early and never came back. In his relationships, he repeatedly left women feeling as rejected as he had felt in his growing-up years, a common way of dealing with loss and psychological trauma.

Clearly, Jesse's difficulty with commitment was connected to the entire history of his childhood. If you are a Jesse, psychotherapy to heal the deep root causes of your anxiety may be important—not only so you can make the step of commitment, but to enable you to stay fully engaged in your relationship.

Fear of Accepting Life in the Here and Now

Sometimes anxiety over connection results from anger over aspects of the life your lover marries you to—the environment that he brings to you.

Life is a package deal, and your love relationship defines much of your package. Whom you marry, for instance, determines whether you have children, and what those children will be like. Your choice of mate may well influence or determine where you live, your financial status, your career options, and your friends. The package that develops over time often contains elements that you really love, and elements that may be difficult to accept.

When elements of your life cause you frustration (and when are there not?), you may respond in two ways. The first is to turn away from life in the here and now and indulge in fantasies of what a different life might be like. That "different life" might be the life you once had. It might be the life you hope to create in the future. It might be the life your best friend has. But it's not *your* life *right now*.

When you feel unable to change frustrating aspects of you're here-and-now life, you will often feel tempted to direct your resentment toward your other. You may not be able to express your discontent toward your boss, but you can blame the husband whose job ties you to the city in which you live. You may not be able to correct your child's behavior, but you can resent your spouse for not being a better parent. You may not be able to create the affluent lifestyle of your sister or your best friend, but you can feel frustrated that your mate is not a stronger wage earner. That frustration damages your ability for loving connection with your mate. The fabric of your relationship is strained and may begin to tear—unfortunately, since your relationship is not the source of your feelings.

There are many variations on the theme of pushing away love in the here and now:

Fran was deeply resentful of her husband's long hours, the pressures of his job, and that his work tied them to a city that she disliked. Her response was to continually dream of the day they would retire, and she focused all her emotional energy on building toward the life they would someday have together. She did, however, enjoy the wealthy material lifestyle his work afforded them, and on several occasions when her husband proposed moving to a more desirable location where he could have a less pressured job, she resisted. Her husband eventually burned out both on his job and on her continual resentment and left the marriage. Fran spent the next few years preoccupied with mourning "the life I once had" rather than working to build a new life for herself.

Geannie came to see me because of chronic depression and dissatisfaction with her life. She, too, was angry at her husband because his job tied them to a city that was far from her hometown where her parents and sister lived. "If only I'd insisted we stay in my hometown!" She was also preoccupied with social problems her two sons were having in school. Both of them were overweight and endlessly teased by their classmates. "Obesity runs in my husband's family. If I'd married someone else, they wouldn't have this problem!" she lamented to me on a number of occasions. A third issue was money; her husband worked as a principal, earning a moderate income, but many of her friends lived more affluently. "If only I'd married my first boyfriend—he's loaded!"

Then there was Phil. His anxiety about "the package deal" was anticipatory. He had been badly burned in his first marriage, and though he loved the children the marriage had produced, he resented paying child support and alimony to his first wife. On three successive occasions he had dated women who might have been suitable wives, women he actually cared for a great deal. But his mind was plagued with what-if: "What if I get married, and we have more children, and the marriage falls apart, and I get stuck again with shelling out a lot of money?" Never mind that in truth he had plenty of money, that he really enjoyed children, and that he was quite unhappy when each of these relationships broke up. Because he dreaded the "package," he was terrified of committing to a permanent connection.

Using the Future to Protect Yourself from the Present

Another pattern of avoiding life in the here and now is to erect a fantasy of how life will be "someday" while avoiding the hard work of real change today. Carla, mother of a teenage daughter, lamented her solitary life but told her friends that after her daughter was grown, she would start dating. In the meantime she avoided opportunities to date and let her physical appearance slide. She neither allowed herself to truly enjoy her current life nor would she take active steps toward what might be a richer life. Why? By not taking social risks, she avoided risking her self-esteem; she had been badly wounded in her previous marriage and was terrified to trust another man. But by living in a world of "someday" she also avoided confronting the limitations she had placed on her own happiness.

"If only . . ." "Why can't he just . . ." "Maybe someday . . ." "In my old life . . ." The language of resentment is the expression of refusal to accept responsibility for living in the here and now. The past is over. The future may never come. Other places are far away. Other people's children are not yours. Your financial limitations are your current reality. To use those issues to damage your capacity for loving connection is to wish your life away.

Yes, your relationship does connect you to a host of reality issues. But any other relationship would as well, and no relationship at all also connects you to challenges and frustrations. You challenge is to stop looking over your shoulder at what might have been and ask the only question that really matters: How can you live most fully in the here and now? How can you stop blaming your other for your unhappiness and accept full responsibility for the life you have created for yourself?

The more responsibility you accept for your own happiness, the less burden you will place on your relationship, and the more loving your relationship can become.

Fear of Sexual Connection

One way in which males and females do differ is in the use of sexuality to establish connection. Because of the powerful effects of testosterone, men often maintain their sex drive within a marriage even when emotional closeness has been weakened. For women, the thread of sexual connection is far more easily broken when emotional intimacy has been strained.

Further, many women say that issues not related to emotional intimacy may disrupt their sexual interest. One of the most common is the birth of a baby; it is not rare for a woman to report a major shutdown of sexual interest in her husband despite continuing to love her mate. Another time of shutdown is during menopause, when hormonal changes including difficulty with vaginal lubrication and thinning of the vaginal wall may affect sexuality. Sometimes hormone replacement therapy, particularly with small doses of testosterone, can be helpful. A third reason that women lose interest in sex is weight gain. While men don't seem to be troubled by their own pregnant abdomens, women often stop seeing themselves as erotic beings when their waistline expands.

If you are a woman who has had a long-term (or even lifelong) decrease in sexual interest, is it possible to reawaken sexually? Absolutely. *The challenge is to unleash your erotic imagination.* I have yet to meet a person who did not have an erotic fantasy somewhere, even if it had long been sequestered away under layers of neglect and discomfort. *Where has yours gone?*

The drive of testosterone coupled with gender-based cultural expectations makes it far easier for men to retain conscious access to their erotic fantasies. For women, a host of issues drives their sexual imagination underground. We have a societal Madonna-whore complex; "good" women aren't sexy, and sexy women aren't "good." While society is permissive about young women's sexual provocativeness, middle-aged and older women are made to feel that their sexuality is ridiculous or degrading. There are particularly harsh and belittling messages about overweight women as sexual beings. As the majority of American women are now overweight, we have the unfortunate paradox of a sexually permissive society in which the majority of women feel sexually undesirable.

Sexual shutdown may take a variety of forms. At the most concrete level, you may find yourself rarely or never having sexual intercourse. But shutdown may also take the form of hiding your sexual attractiveness by neglecting your appearance or choosing only unflattering or gender-neutral clothes, shoes, and hairstyles. It may take the form of avoiding flirtatious behavior with a real or potential mate. It may take the form of avoiding sexually charged ideas or never masturbating.

If you've shut down sexually, getting to the heart of the matter requires you to reawaken your eroticism. There are specific steps you can take:

1. Give yourself permission to "think sexy."

2. Share your erotic imagination with your lover.

3. Create the conditions that promote eroticism.

Thinking "Sexy"

You may have grown up with parents who made you uncomfortable with your sexuality. Perhaps your religion is critical of eroticism. You may be worried about being criticized or laughed at by others if you are sexy. All of those concerns block the natural flow of sexual energy within you.

Giving yourself permission to be sexual can and should take many forms. You may choose to dress more attractively, to buy those strappy high heels, a low-cut sweater for evening wear, or a sheer negligee for bedtime. You may read sexually charged material or look at videos. You may indulge in masturbatory fantasies that really stimulate you. Give yourself permission to think and feel absolutely whatever you please, whatever lights your fire. Remember that all those thoughts are simply going on within your own mind. No one else knows.

When I was in medical school many years ago, we took a course in behavioral science that included a segment entitled "Human Sexuality." (The title itself spoke to significant discomfort with the subject, for no other course had to be labeled "human" to seem more scientific. What other kind of sexuality would one study in medical school?)

Part of this course was so-called desensitization, and our instructors brought in some graphic videos for us to watch. I, ignorant of the topic of the day, walked into the class late and had to stand in the back of the mostly male class while the video of a naked man lying on the floor masturbating played. However, I had not worn my glasses that day and couldn't see it too clearly. Raising my hand, I asked, "Is he having a grand mal seizure?"

I hope you're more knowledgeable about so-called human sexuality than I was, and that you know the difference between orgasmic ecstasy and status epilepticus. But in retrospect, it was helpful to go through that so-called desensitization, for I became much more comfortable with sex. If you sense that you have lingering discomfort with sex, or if you'd simply like to learn more about an important topic, create your own "human sexuality" course. Go to the bookstore and read some of the excellent and explicit books you'll find. Find videos that help you learn more about eroticism. Talk with friends about their experiences. Your goal is to desensitize yourself to sexual anxiety—and to sensitize yourself to sexual connection.

Communicating Your Erotic Desires with Your Lover

Turning erotic fantasies into actual behavior requires a high level of trust between you and your mate. You both need to be able to verbally express what turns you on without fear of being rejected, laughed at, or disapproved of. That level of trust doesn't begin in the bedroom. You and your mate may need to work on trust in your everyday life with less emotionally charged situations. How do you respond to each other when you express sensitive issues? How often and with what words do you criticize each other? What are the ways you create the emotional closeness that is the precursor to physical intimacy?

People enact in their sexual relationship whatever their emotional dynamics are. Couples who are competitive with each other compete in bed. Couples who are controlling of each other are controlling in bed. Couples who are mean to each other have sadomasochistic undertones to their sex life. Couples who can't talk or trust each in daily life don't communicate in bed. *You do physically what you feel emotionally.*

So work on trust issues with your mate. Tell him that you'd like to set an explicit goal of deepening trust, and ask him what you could do to increase his ability to trust you with his feelings. Share with him what he could do to make it easier for you to be vulnerable. Tell him that your eventual goal is to improve your sex life together. And remember that the core activity of building trust is simple listening.

As trust builds, your ability to share your erotic imagination will also develop. It's impossible to have a great sex life without talking about it. You have to be able to tell him what pleases you. He has to be able to ask you for what he wants. Human beings are highly idiosyncratic in how they respond sexually, and no one can understand you unless you talk to them.

Women are able to understand male sexuality far more easily than men can understand women's responsiveness for the simple reason that the erect penis is a tip-off. Most men are clueless about female sexuality but are desperate to learn. They don't know where the clitoris is, much less how to stimulate it. They believe that nipple erection is proof that a woman is sexually excited. They don't know that the upper two-thirds of the vagina has limited sensation and that sexual excitement centers in the clitoris. They think that a penis in the vagina is necessary for orgasm, and it hurts their feelings when they learn otherwise. They have no way of knowing if a woman is becoming turned on unless she lets him know verbally.

So why don't men know these things? Because we don't tell

them. It's not their fault, it's our fault, ladies. How in the world can your mate understand your sexuality if you don't tell him about it?

Start talking.

Creating the Conditions That Promote Romance and Eroticism

Many, maybe most, women experience their sexuality only in certain contexts. If you are aware that particular conditions promote your responsiveness, create those conditions. Warm up the room so that you're comfortable naked. Set the lighting to create romance. While some of these conditions may be environmental—time of day, lighting, location, and so forth—others are probably experiential. Maybe you need a quiet evening with after-dinner dancing in the living room. Maybe taking a warm shower with your mate does it for you. Perhaps the two of you get turned on by watching a sexy movie. Or by getting a sitter and going out to dinner together.

Consider as well the emotional conditions you need for lovemaking. Certain conditions are anti-aphrodisiacs:

- Arguing

- Exhaustion

- Stress and tension

- Intoxication

- Resentment

- Lack of privacy

The most powerful anti-aphrodisiacs of all are your bundles of joy. It's a droll joke of nature that conception starts with sexual passion, for nothing then kills eroticism like a baby. If you have trouble reestablishing your sex life after the birth of your infant, ask your mother or sister to baby-sit your child overnight to give you and your husband a chance to reconnect. Do not start sleeping with your child. Not only is it unsafe for your child, but it is a proven way to kill your sex life.

The most important condition of all to set is your imagination. All of us have particular images or fantasies that are sexually exciting. If you haven't indulged yourself in those for a long time, remember back to what turned you on as a young person. It is said that men are more responsive to visual stimuli than women. I'm not sure that is so, for it may just be that men have long been given a wide range of visual stimuli to respond to, and social permission to be aroused in that way. Whether your erotic stimuli are visual or behavioral, focus on them. Bring them to bed with you.

Rebalancing Your Life

When your zone of interpersonal safety becomes small, you will seek to fill up the void in your life in other ways. The more you block out love, the more you will search for alternative activities to structure your day, shore up your self-esteem, and give your life a sense of meaning. Those alternative activities may be inherently worthy and genuinely fulfilling and in the right doses are part of a wonderful, balanced life. The challenge is to determine when you have achieved the right balance—and when you are using those activities to avoid seeking or maintaining intimate love.

The Hypertrophied Mom

One of the most common ways that a woman's life becomes unbalanced in a way that damages spousal love is through overly intense preoccupation with motherhood. Motherhood is, after all, such a wonderful experience. Can it be possible to be too good a mother? Trina M told me how:

"When I was growing up, my mother was totally devoted to the family. In fact, she still is, to this day. *Every* moment of her life was spent trying to figure out ways to make our lives better, how to make us happy. The sad thing is, we're not happy. I've had lifelong trouble with depression, and my brother has never been able to hold down a job. I really think her love was toxic, though she would say she'd cut off her right arm for us.

"Maybe in fact that's the problem. I didn't really want to be responsible for my mother's right arm.

"I'll give you an example. When I was a teenager, I was overweight—maybe twenty-five pounds or so, but that's a big deal for a teenager. I knew my mother couldn't stand it, because it meant that maybe I wasn't happy, and also that I would have a hard time getting a boyfriend. So she did everything in the world to try to fix it without ever talking directly about it. She'd spend hours cooking gourmet, low-fat meals, and she'd always be trying in roundabout ways to get me to exercise. But she also didn't want me to have to bear the consequences of being fat by going to a store and trying on clothes that wouldn't fit, so she spent a huge amount of time sewing clothes for me that she thought would be flattering.

"The worst was when I would get invited to parties. I hated going—I'd so much rather just stay home—but I knew my mother would have been so worried and upset if I didn't have a social life. So she would sit up into the wee hours, sewing a party dress for me that didn't emphasize my weight. And then I'd dutifully go to the party, but I'd always just go into the bathroom and sit, sometimes for hours. I never told her how much I hated those parties.

"To this day all this stuff still goes on. Last week I told her my son had lost his mittens, so by the next day she had knitted him a new pair, with his name knitted into the pattern. And of course I have to talk to her every day, because I know how happy it makes her. I love her, but I hate feeling like I'm the center of her life. It means I can't be the center of my own life."

If I could have talked to Trina's mother, Mrs. M, I'm sure she would have said something like "But all I ever wanted was for Trina to be happy! I'd have done *anything* for my family!"

I might counter, "*Anything* except stop suffocating them with your 'love' so that they might live their own lives without guilt and resentment." What Mrs. M called "love" was so exaggerated that it was really a means to control her family, to ensure that she herself was always at the center of the family life. Mrs. M had deep, understandable anxieties about abandonment, for her own parents had died when she was a child and she was raised by a series of relatives. Her response was to say, "I don't ever want my child to feel as unloved as I felt." Her real fear was "*I* don't ever want to feel unloved again." She was terrified of rejection and orchestrated family dynamics around her own terror.

A central question for Mrs. M is "Why have you married your children instead of your husband?" Her overinvolvement with her kids solved a number of psychological problems for her. Scared of intimacy with her husband, she had found love and emotional nourishment in her children. As a mother, she found a reliable source of self-esteem. After all, the nobility of motherhood is unassailable. How could either her children or her husband fault her when she was such a caring, unselfish person?

An old concept in psychoanalytic theory is called the "good enough mother." The notion is that a child doesn't need, and really shouldn't have, a perfect mother, for every child needs to learn to cope with the frustration of imperfect parents in order to grow up and eventually leave the nest. Good enough is good enough; suffocating a child with love is like drowning a seedling with too much water.

Watch the young mother of a newborn and you will usually see a woman in love . . . with a baby. It's a wonderful thing to behold, and even more wonderful to experience. But there comes the time when it's time to step back from that "in love" experience, to refall in love with your husband, and to allow your baby to grow and leave your side.

Hypertrophied Work

Another way to avoid intimacy is by immersing yourself excessively in work. When family life is too stressful, when you and your mate just can't connect anymore, or when the thought of dating is just too frightening, work waits patiently for you, offering endless excuses to avoid intimacy. Humans may reject you, but work will never reject you. Home life may be unrewarding, but work offers a paycheck. You may have forgotten how to play, but work will fill your time. You may have lost your spirituality, but work makes you feel worthwhile.

Work is a good thing—but it's possible to have too much of a good thing, as the marriage of Doug and Jan illustrates. Doug and Jan met in college. They were more drawn toward each other for their differences than their similarities, for Doug was warm and extroverted, while Jan was quiet and somewhat mysterious to Doug. A few years after graduation they married. Both worked hard at their jobs, saving for their first home. They bought the home, and three children followed during the next years. Doug began to feel the financial pressures of supporting the family and worked hard at his job as a salesman for a computer firm. Jan began to feel overwhelmed by sustaining a job and raising three children, and they mutually decided that she would stay home.

Both Doug and Jan were really good at their respective areas of work, perhaps too good. Doug became highly successful as a salesman and earned large commissions for his computer sales to major corporations. He traveled increasingly and saw his family mainly on weekends. In the back of his mind he felt vaguely uneasy about being absent so much of the time, but the lure of just one more big sale made it hard for him to set limits on his time away from home. Jan, on the other hand, was an extremely devoted, organized homemaker. The house was meticulously maintained, the children always arrived on time for their many after-school activities, and she learned to function quite well in Doug's absence. In fact, she functioned so well with the children that she found Doug somewhat in the way when he was home. Their relationship became emotionally flat. They had perfunctory sex once a week on Saturday nights whether they felt like it or not. They bickered occasionally, though not excessively—they were more likely to withdraw rather than confront each other over conflicts. Over the years the problem in the marriage was not so much what did happen, but what didn't happen, for there was little conversation, affection, or genuine enjoyment of each other. Their safety zone of loving interaction had been squeezed down by their lives of duty and responsibility.

It wasn't that either of them consciously thought, "Gee, I'll work really hard in order to avoid dealing with my mate." The process of their detachment was much more subtle. For Doug, work was fun and rewarding, and home life was just uncomfortable enough that he never felt true desire to work less and stay home more. For Jan, there just wasn't enough interaction with Doug when he was home to keep her wanting to be near him; there was always a children's activity, a bit of housework, or bills waiting to be paid that kept her busy and unengaged with Doug.

Not only love got short shrift in their lives; they had quite literally forgotten how to have fun. Americans have become so excessively preoccupied with work that we hardly know how to enjoy ourselves. The less you are involved with such pleasures as exercise, hobbies, friendships, the less competent you become at those activities. A vicious cycle develops of working more, enjoying less, and being literally less able *to* enjoy. Such was the case for Doug and Jan.

The solution? Set extremely concrete limits on work life, rules that are inviolable except under extreme circumstances. Precisely how you set those rules is up to you: Maybe it's *No housework after 2 P.M.* Or, *No more than one overnight business trip per week.* Or, *No work on the weekends.* But without rules there will be no home life.

Healing Your Connection Anxiety

You can start today to improve your ability to love by healing the anxiety that makes you disconnect from others. But you won't finish today, nor tomorrow, nor this year. Learning to love more deeply is a lifelong process, and the process of opening up your heart to another can continue as long as you live.

But you can begin to make tangible, observable progress immediately to make more room for love in your heart.

1. Observe Yourself

Observe your behavior and the impact of what you say and do has on others. Notice how when you are loving and open, others instantly become more so as well. Notice also how when you're tense and withdrawn, others are, too.

Just as a dog will bite when it is scared, humans become reactive and belligerent when we feel threatened. Pay particular attention to what makes you angry, for under anger there is always anxiety. The things that make you angriest reveal what you're most afraid of.

Every once in a while I'll have someone in therapy pour out a litany of problems and then reject every insight I can think of. A simple intervention often breaks through the impasse. "Okay," I'll say, "let's pretend you were the therapist sitting in that chair over there. If you were listening to all of this, what would you say?" Almost invariably my patient will be able to offer himself or herself remarkably insightful, often very confrontational comments.

So practice being your own therapist. Listen to yourself talk, watch yourself in action. Then pause, reflect, and ask, if I were the therapist, what would I have to say about all of this?

2. Face Up to Your Woozle of Hostile Intent

Of all the difficult people you will ever have to deal with in your life, you are the most difficult, for you are the one person you can never get away from. You are more difficult—to you—than everyone else put together, because you control how all other people relate to you. The more you are able to be honest about your motives and behavior, the easier it will be to find love. The more you are able to understand the distorting effect your unconscious anxiety has on your perceptions and interpersonal behavior, the sooner you will be able to change.

That's easier said than done because most of us try to control others rather than seeing ourselves clearly. Because of the power of self-deception, it's easier to learn about yourself by indirect, rather than direct, means. Like the hunter who looks for game by searching for paw prints in the forest ground, you can find the most useful information about yourself by examining the trail you have left behind as you've walked through life. Your trail allows you to see the major patterns of your life.

Most of us are like Winnie-the-Pooh tracking Woozles of Hostile Intent in the forest. Filled with trepidation, Pooh began to follow the tracks of the feared Woozle. After a while, the tracks were joined by those of a second Woozle, and finally a third and a fourth. Finally Pooh got it: he was following his own tracks.

The process of growing emotionally is much like that for we all have Woozles of Hostile Intent within ourselves. The first difficult relationship you have you blame on your other. And maybe the second as well. But in time, you begin to suspect that you are following your own tracks, and that if you're ever going to get anywhere, you must stop chasing yourself.

3. Discuss Your Personal Issues with Someone You Trust

This is one of the most important parts of expanding your safety zone. Talking is a miraculous process. When you thoughtfully discuss an important emotional issue, you have the opportunity to reprogram your mind. You can block your automatic behavioral patterns. You can disengage the issue from the ingrained, reflexive emotions associated with it. Talking is your mind's immune system, neutralizing toxic anxiety just as your antibodies surround and deactivate microbes in your physical body.

If you're having a connection problem with someone you love, the best person to talk to about it is that person. If you're like most people, you shy away from doing that, afraid to expose your vulnerability. You may believe that if you don't talk about your dysfunctional interactions, no one else will notice. Remind yourself that you're probably the last person to notice, and your other is likely to be thrilled by your honest effort to improve the relationship.

Perhaps you're afraid that if you try to change, your other won't change and you'll have done all the work by yourself. In fact, your other may not change, but don't try to grow in an attempt to change him or her. Grow your heart for your own sake.

One woman I treated in couples therapy was fond of saying to her husband, "Say it to me, dear: 'You're always right.'" Predictably, his desire to communicate meaningfully to her shut down completely. Set the stage for dialogue with the opposite words: "I may be wrong about this. Tell me how you see it." Humor, honesty, and humility are the three magic ingredients of loving communication.

Discussion is not a onetime event. It's a way of life in a loving relationship. Make it a practice to have frequent "check-ins" with your mate to see how things are going and to get feedback. If you're not in a relationship, discussing your issues is still critically important. A close friend may be a good choice for dialogue, particularly if he or she also has issues to work on. If you don't have a close friend or if the intensity of your connection problems is significant, find a good therapist. Set your goals, stay on target, and work hard until you see real progress.

4. Lay Out a Plan

How will you know if you're making progress? After you've observed, owned, and discussed your issue, what concrete steps can you take daily that will keep you on track and become markers of reaching your goals?

Drew, a busy executive, became aware that he was always so focused on his productivity that his relationships were becoming sorely strained. He laid out a simple plan for himself, with three concrete behaviors. He began to make it a point every day to encourage someone, to thank someone, and to share a belly laugh with someone.

Sharon, a working mother, realized that she felt disconnected from the rest of the family. Everyone was so busy rushing off that there was no time for close conversation. She laid out a simple plan: spend at least ten minutes every day listening carefully to each member of her family individually. Her sense of closeness to her family members improved significantly, and she found that no one wanted to limit the time to just ten minutes.

Janet felt that she had become romantically disconnected from her husband. In fact, she had ceased to think of herself as a sexual being at all. Her plan also consisted of a few simple behaviors: She decided to dress attractively every day. She set aside the last hour of every evening as quiet time with her husband, with the opportunity for sex when they felt like it. And she hired a baby-sitter for Saturday nights so that she and her husband could have some fun together each week. Although Janet had conceptualized her plan as a way for her to change, what she observed were the changes in her husband, who became much more engaged, affectionate, and thoughtful toward her. He began to help with child care and housework more, and she found that she had more time, not less, for relaxation.

Denise had been divorced for five years and had not had a date in two years. Realizing that she was becoming increasingly socially isolated, her plan was to make it a practice to smile and make eye contact with people she passed at work; engage in one activity each weekend that got her out of the house and into the company of others; and take a trip once a year to a setting where she might meet people. Eventually she met a man and began to date him. Although she did not wish to marry him, she felt increasingly confident in herself and content in her lifestyle.

Laying out a plan and sticking to it is key. It will do you no good at all to understand and explore your problem if you don't take concrete steps to fix it.

5. *Experiment with New Strategies*

Often when I make a suggestion to a therapy patient about a way to break through his or her isolation, I will hear a flat "Well, I tried that. It didn't work." Huh? Tried "it" once and you didn't meet your soul mate? Tried "it" for a year back in 1996 and haven't left your home on a weekend since then? Tried "it" with your first husband and have therefore written off the remaining 2 billion men?

When a scientist conducts an experiment, by definition she's not really sure how it's going to turn out. She's simply trying a certain procedure under some set of conditions to see what might happen. If the experiment "fails," she doesn't immediately assume that her assumptions were wrong; rather, she tries it out a few more times. She might then try changing the conditions of the experiment to see if that will make a difference. She knows that the first time she conducts the experiment, she's not going to win the Nobel Prize. She commits herself to a long process of trial and error, always aiming toward her goal. If she's a good scientist, she's not easily discouraged or fatigued by failure. She keeps on experimenting and through the process learns a great deal.

Think of yourself as an experimenter. If you try out a new behavior and you don't immediately get the results you desire, don't give up. Try a few dozen—no, a few hundred—more times and see what happens. Keep changing your conditions until you learn what makes a difference. Keep trying.

6. *Savor the Journey*

And as you're trying, have fun. Don't wish your life away by seeing the present as simply a holding pattern until better times come. Your efforts to connect should be fun, not a grim war to be fought. Don't take yourself so seriously that you see every interaction as the proof of whether you're a good person or whether life is worth living. Don't use one particular relationship to judge the nature of mankind.

Try as well not to have one highly specific goal—e.g., getting married—as the proof of whether you're making progress. You may dramatically expand your safety zone and still have to wait a while to meet the right person. Further, if you do meet that one person, you will still be challenged for the rest of your life to connect deeply and lovingly.

Some issues in your life you cannot magically control. You can't make your soul mate walk through the door just because you're now ready for him. But many parts of your life you can control, all of which define the quality of your daily life. It's always possible to laugh more spontaneously, to understand more clearly, and to appreciate your world more fully. It's always possible to open your heart more widely to those around you. And it's always possible to let more fresh air and sunshine into the room where you live your entire life—the safety zone that exists within your mind.

CHAPTER FIVE

Establish Emotional Independence

IF YOU THINK MORE DEEPLY about your safety zone, you'll notice that over time it shrinks and expands in size, maybe even in a few hours. Think back to the last time you and your other argued. Perhaps the conversation started off pleasantly enough; you were both feeling comfortable, engaged peaceably or even lovingly with each other. Then something happened. Maybe your other said something irritating, and you wanted to make just one little comment to straighten things out, like dabbing a bit of paint on a chipped place on the wall. But suddenly you dropped the whole can of paint and it splattered everywhere. You triggered something that made him or her return a real stinger. You yowled, and the fight was off and running. The evening was ruined, and you're not quite sure how it all happened.

At the moment the two of you evacuated your safety zones, something dramatic happened. You became a different you—no longer serene and loving, but defensive and angry. You suddenly saw your other in a different light. Where only moments before you experienced him or her as a pleasant, loving companion, suddenly you remembered all of the irritating, disappointing traits you usually ignore. Your mood changed dramatically as well. Your sunny, balmy sense of well-being was replaced with irritability and then resentment.

How could such a psychological metamorphosis have occurred? To understand it better, let's look at a related phenomenon: multiple personality disorder.

Multiple Personalities

Within the past two decades, multiple personality disorder has received a good deal of attention in the psychiatric community and the lay press. The vast majority of those suffering from multiple personality disorder—MPD—are women who have been terribly abused as children and have developed the ability to "split off" portions of their personality into specific alter identities. An alter acts like a template or pattern that temporarily defines one's feelings and behavior in a relationship. While in an alter the woman adopts a specific identity quite different from her own. She may become a different age, nationality, or the opposite gender. (I once treated a woman with an alter who was a cat!) Each alter perceives others in a specifc, distorted way, such as seeing all men as abusive. In the alter personality the woman displays a particular mood, such as anger, withdrawal, or seductivness. Notably, she will often have amnesia for what occurred while in the alter state.

This phenomenon sounds truly bizarre. How in the world can several personalities exist within the same brain? You might think of an alter as simply a complex, highly defined pattern of perceiving a relationship. The person with MPD has distorted her mental images of her "self" and her "other" to an exaggerated degree in order to deal with emotional pain. This is an extreme version of what we all do when strong emotions color our perceptions.

And like the person with MPD, you can also observe that you

and your other will have partial amnesia, or at least a distorted memory of the event. After several weeks, if the two of you recall the incident, you may come up with something like:

HE: Remember when you said you hated me when I acted like that?

YOU: I didn't say I hated you! I might have said I hated *it*, but not you! But what about when you said I was just like my mother and you really couldn't stand it when—

HE: That was not what I said. I remember I chose my words very carefully. I said that I understood it was normal in your family to act like that, but I just wasn't used to it. I was just trying to say that I accepted we had different backgrounds, not that yours was wrong and mine was right.

Who's right? Who knows? Both of you have a distorted memory of how you really behaved and what you really said. But during that argument, unconscious anxiety was triggered. Perhaps it was the anxiety that you'd be attacked. Perhaps it was fear that you'd be out of control. Maybe you were scared that you'd be abandoned. Whatever the nature of your unconscious anxiety, the two of you foisted roles on each other and yourselves. A template for interaction was activated in which you each:

• Experienced different perceptions of your "self" at that moment.

• Perceived your other in very different ways from your normal perceptions.

• Felt overwhelmed by distinct and unusual emotions that colored your interaction.

As you read these words, you are probably mildly to moderately convinced that what I am describing applies to you. It is hard to perceive templates within yourself for any number of reasons. Your human mind naturally wants to rationalize your responses and behaviors. Your innate tendency will always be to justify your actions on the basis of others' provocations. Anybody would have responded the way I did, given the circumstances!

But the denial of your own templates goes deeper than that. The templates are always triggered by powerful emotions, and emotions in and of themselves cause you to alter your image of yourself and of others. Strong emotions of any type limit your capacity to observe yourself and distort your memory of events.

Every human personality contains a collection of templates unique to that individual. While some of your templates are healthy and life-affirming, others keep you from getting the love you want by poisoning your interaction. There is a marked difference between the templates you experience in your safety zone and those that are triggered by connection anxiety.

An example:

> **ELIZABETH** *(in her safety zone):* "I really love being a wife and taking care of my family. My husband appreciates what I do and works hard himself for the sake of all of us. I feel fulfilled and at peace with my choice."

> **ELIZABETH** *(experiencing connection anxiety):* "I'm the family drudge who has sacrificed her life for the sake of the family. No one notices what I do, no one cares, and my husband takes advantage of me by working long hours and expecting me to pick up the pieces at home. I really gave up a lot when I decided to stop working and stay home."

These words were actually spoken at two different times by the same woman, Elizabeth. What triggered the transformation of perception? Elizabeth's husband had decided to go hunting for a weekend with his buddies, and she was upset that he hadn't thought to suggest that the two of them go away for a weekend together instead. The entire weekend of his absence she fumed.

Another example:

> **HEIDI** *(in her safety zone):* "I feel really good about myself. I know I'm a fun person that people want to be around, and when my husband and I go out together, we always have a good time."
>
> **HEIDI** *(experiencing connection anxiety):* "I've become a fat slug. My husband probably isn't attracted to me any-more and I can hardly stand to look at myself in the mirror. We haven't had sex in a while, but I can't stand the thought of him looking at me undressed."

These were Heidi's thoughts, before and after going to a party at which her husband's first wife showed up wearing a sexy dress that showed off that she had lost considerable weight.

While it's easy to understand the all-too-human feelings that Elizabeth and Heidi had, they nonetheless paid an emotional price for their reactions and dynamics in their marriages. Elizabeth didn't have to wait for her husband to plan a weekend for the two of them. She could have made those plans herself, but was habitually passive, not taking the initiative. Further, she had girlfriends with whom she might plan a weekend away, but had never taken time away from the family. Heidi's husband was actually baffled by her emotional shutdown after the party. He really loved her, and while he knew she needed to lose a few pounds, he still found her attractive and was always ready, willing, and able to enjoy sex with her.

What each of these women had done was to make her emotional well-being dependent on the behavior or feelings—or even imagined feelings—of her other. Each could have saved herself considerable unhappiness by establishing her own emotional independence and creating the conditions she needed to maintain her own happiness and self-esteem.

What Is Emotional Independence?

Emotional independence is both a state of mind and a philosophy of life in which you hold yourself responsible for your own happiness and welfare moment by moment.

As a state of mind, emotional independence allows you to stay in your safety zone. You stop asking others to regulate your self-esteem, for you understand that only you can give yourself ultimate approval. You relieve others from the burden of managing your moods. You stop expecting your other to read your mind and divine what you want. You think less often in terms of phrases like "You make me mad" or "You make me happy" and become more interested in observing and occasionally challenging your own reactions.

As a philosophy, emotional independence teaches you to accept that not only you but each person in your life has ultimate responsibility for his or her life. You accept that you will never be able to help another person more than he can help himself, so you try to encourage and facilitate, rather than fix and prop up, the lives of others. You wish to be the shepherd of your own life, for at the end of the day it is up to you to make your own choices. You are neither a victim nor a bystander in your own life.

It's a lofty ideal, isn't it? Realistically, much as you'd love to become emotionally independent today, emotional independence lies at the core of the lifelong process of acquiring wisdom and maturity. Maturation is not linear but oscillating: three steps forward, two back. You may have a jarring experience and react by stepping into an alter, activating a template of distorted perceptions of your self and your other. But then you pause. You're quiet for a few moments, thinking rather than popping off. You ask yourself to take a time-out. You decide to own your mood of the moment, and you reestablish a more whole and valid sense of your self and of your other. And that's real emotional growth.

The Central Importance of Boundaries

The notion of emotional boundaries is old, but is usually used in a way that limits the richness of the concept. Common usage of the term *boundary violation* means that someone has butted in where he doesn't belong, violating your privacy or autonomy. I want you to think of boundaries from a different perspective: What are the boundaries you need to observe from both sides? Your boundaries determine the psychological territory outside of which you will not intrude, and they also determine the space within you that you must not allow or expect others to be responsible for.

When you clearly demarcate territory that is off-limits to you, you free your other to have a more independent life without worrying about your reaction. You accept that no matter how intimate your relationship is, some areas of his or her life are off-limits to you. Some concrete examples include:

- Relationships with his family

- His personal friendships

- His personal spending money

- Time designated as his free time

- His work relationships
- His personal possessions
- His health practices
- His private thoughts

I can hear your protest, but what about the ways those things impact my life? What if he spends so much time with his buddies that he has no time for me? What if his poor health habits mean I'll end up a widow? What if I can see that he's making bad decisions at work that will affect our future? What about the fact that I have to go to his family's get-togethers?

Rights in a relationship aren't carved on a tablet somewhere; they're only practices that you and your other agree on. So, yes, you can certainly claim the right to discuss all of those concerns with your other, particularly if asked. If you must, feel free to blast your way into trying to dictate how he handles those areas. It's entirely up to you. But it's not emotional independence. Remember two things. First, in the final analysis, he, not you, has the ultimate say in how he comports himself in those areas. Second, the more you enter into those areas, the bigger the price you'll pay in your own emotional well-being. You'll find yourself tied up in knots over issues you can't control. You'll spend so much time focusing on his problems that you will neglect your own emotional growth. And you'll stir up so much resentment from him that the very relationship you're supposed to be trying to strengthen will become weaker.

In areas where his personal behaviors intersect with your relationship, you have "the right" to address that intersection only insofar as it directly affects you or your relationship. Therefore, you may choose to:

- Not go to his family get-togethers if they upset you, so long as he is able to go himself

- Work together to budget family money, so long as you each have some individual discretionary money

- Plan vacations and recreational time together, but not forbid him to take time away from the family

- Ask him to be tidy in the family common living area, so long as he has some space that is his

- Discuss his work issues with him, but not dictate the decisions he makes

And obviously, the same holds true about his behavior toward you.

The other direction of establishing your boundaries is from the outside in, a delineation of those emotional areas that are off-limits to others. It isn't just that others don't have a right to intrude; more importantly, you should not expect others to step in. Some of those areas include:

- Regulation of your self-esteem

- Regulation of your mood

- Decisions about your personal development, e.g., education

- Initiation of activities that give structure to your life

- Negotiating your relationships with your family and personal friends

- Control of your own personal spending money

- Control of your own personal time

Again you protest: But don't I have a right to ask my other to do the things that would make me happy? Doesn't he have the right to share his opinion about important decisions in my life?

Again, you each have whatever rights you mutually grant each other. But remember, the more you give him responsibility to make you happy, the less control you have over your own emotional well-being. The greater the expectations you have that he will give you a life, the more you will resent his failure to do so. The more you ask him to influence your thinking about your personal issues, the less room you'll have to explore your own desires.

As you practice emotional independence, you'll notice a change in many small behaviors. You'll watch yourself begin to:

- Plan rather than wait

- Express yourself rather than expect to have your mind read

- Ask questions rather than guess your other's feelings

- Feel responsible for your own moods rather than blame external events

- See yourself as an actor rather than a victim

- Observe rather than control others

- Allow others to find their way rather than rush to protect them

- Allow yourself to make mistakes without an orgy of self-blame

- Stabilize your self-esteem rather than seek admiration

- Feel admiration rather than envy for others

- Engage rather than cling

- Thoughtfully choose friends rather than "fall in" with people
- Establish your own financial goals rather than being financially dependent
- Allocate time for your own activities, rather than simply serve others
- Define your wishes rather than accepting the leftovers

Establishing emotional independence allows you to maintain a steady, reliable sense of self that creates honest, resilient self-esteem. Your sense of humor and humility will improve as well, for when you stop blaming others, you can begin to work on self-acceptance. That, in turn, makes it easier to accept the flaws of your other.

As you reach toward greater emotional independence, try to identify specific interactions that are outside your boundaries. You'll increasingly observe patterns of unhealthy dynamics you tend to set up, and you'll become uncomfortable with the price you pay for those interactions. As you become really wise, you'll hear warning chimes when you're tempted to go outside the boundaries of emotional independence.

Emotional Independence through the Life Cycle of Your Relationship

Different stages in your relationship will challenge your emotional independence in different ways. In the earliest phase of falling in love, the euphoric merger you feel with your beloved is so powerful that you submerge your individuality. After that first passionate phase subsides, you begin to learn about each other as distinct individuals and to establish more honest patterns of communicating. Later, the arrival of children stresses the relationship and forces you to negotiate the division of substantial home responsibilities. Later still, when you've been together for decades rather than years, your challenge is to maintain a fresh view of yourself, your other, and the relationship.

The stresses of each period may make it hard to maintain empathy for each other. The single most common reason why marriages break up is simple selfishness, for it is frighteningly easy to become so absorbed in your own needs that you misinterpret or ignore the needs of others. Emotional independence combined with deep empathy for your other is an antidote to this problem. The former allows you to maintain allegiance to yourself while the latter allows you to stay in love and in tune with your other.

Emotional independence is especially hard to maintain at the moment of meeting someone who might be a candidate for romance. After all, at that moment you're trying to control and direct his or her feelings. If you're attracted, your mental energy becomes so overwhelmed by concern about how you're presenting yourself that there's no room left to consider the feelings of your other. You have an agenda: Look good. Sound smart. Seem hip. Appear available. Don't be threatening. It may so overload your circuits that you feel like a quivering mass of jelly with the IQ of a grape. All of your best traits—your intelligence, your sensitivity, your ability to empathically connect—may dissolve. You may lose the ability to truly engage with your other, and you may not get a second chance.

Missed Opportunities

My patient Ginnie repeatedly blew chances to begin relationships because of her anxiety around men. She could be the life of the party with her girlfriends, but froze when a male appeared. A typical experience:

Ginnie pulled up a chair at a table that was already crowded with four of her girlfriends. "Un-be-liev-able," she said. "You guys wouldn't believe what happened to me today. Picture this. I go to the house of these new clients who wanted me to do over their living room. And dining room. And study. And morning room. And afternoon tea room. You wouldn't believe this place. It's like—I dunno, like something out of West Palm Beach or Hollywood or something. So we're walkin' through this place and I'm really layin' it on, you know, Ms. In-teer-ee-or De-co-ray-tor! I am just too-o-o cool! So then we get to their sunken barroom. But does Ms. In-teer-ee-or De-co-ray-tor see the step down? Oh, no—I'm much too busy pointing up at the vaulted ceiling and the crown moldings! So I slip on the step and go down like a ton of bricks. And these poor people—ohmigod, you should have seen the look on their faces. And I just didn't know what else to do, so I threw up both hands and said, '*Ta-daah!*' " Ginnie threw back her head and howled.

As the laughter at the table subsided, Karen called over to next table in the crowded café, "Jim, get over here. There's some people I want you to meet. This is Susan—you know, she's dating Tom. And this is Kim, who's married to my partner. You know Lisa. And this is Ginnie."

Ginnie stopped laughing. Her face flushed, and she swallowed. "Hi, Jim."

"Hey," Jim said, walking over to the group and smiling broadly. "We're going to go down the block—there's a new band playing at Magruder's. Anyone wanna come?"

All five pairs of eyes turned to Ginnie. She alone was single. The other women all knew that Karen had wanted to hook Ginnie up with Jim. It was the perfect opportunity.

"Actually, I need to get going home. I'm expecting a call tonight."

Jim smiled, waved, and departed. Now four pairs of eyes fastened on Ginnie. "You slug!" hissed Lisa. "It was your perfect opportunity! You're *always* moaning about how you never meet anyone, and now you pass up your golden chance. Jim's such a great guy! What is wrong with you!"

Four days later, Ginnie asked me that question: "What is wrong with me? There I was, having a great time with my girlfriends, like I always do. I'd had a great day. My new clients really liked me—even when I landed on my rear, they thought I was funny. Everyone thinks I'm funny! But when I meet a guy who's a prospect, I just freeze up. My mind goes blank. I can't think of anything to say. What's wrong with me?"

"Who do you become in that moment? How do you see yourself?" I asked.

She sighed, combing her fingers her through her streaked, shoulder-length hair and yanking on a fistful. "I really don't know. All I can think of is, like, 'What is he thinking about me?' I must seem so stupid to him."

At the moment Jim walked up to the table, Ginnie's image of herself changed. Ginnie the cutup, the funny, goofy one who made everyone laugh and yet could nail a great decorating contract because she was really, really good, was transformed in the blink of an eye. Instantaneously she became Ginnie the bland, Ginnie the shy one, the last one to be asked to dance, the one who was always without a boyfriend. At the moment her eyes met Jim's, she might just as well have been put up for sale in the marketplace, eyed and evaluated by a would-be customer, only to be passed over yet again. She experienced her self through the eyes of her other—in this case, Jim—as no longer a person but a commodity.

And yet, what triggered this transformation of her self-image? "When I meet a guy who's a prospect . . ." Huh? Since when is a human being a prospect? A business deal might be a prospect. A piece of real estate might be a prospect. But what not-so-subtle dehumanization turned Jim into a mere prospect?

So what really went on in Ginnie's mind—what were the roles and what was the script she applied to the situation? Was she the "buyer" who quickly sized up Jim, the "goods?" Or was he the buyer and she the goods? The vignette of Ginnie and Jim illustrates a common psychological event that occurs when you activate a template. At first, the emotion of the moment leads you to assign a role to yourself and a complementary role to your other, but these roles are inherently unstable. Your anxiety will often lead you to instantaneously reverse the roles, usually without your being consciously aware that you have made the switch. And when your anxiety triggers a template and you assign a role to the other, you lose true empathy for him or her. You relate to your other not as an individual with his or her own personality, values, and needs, but rather as an extension of your own emotional life. And in so doing, he or she, in turn, will find it more difficult to connect to you. The mutual loss of empathy devastates the development of your relationship.

In Ginnie's case, the "switch" of self and other transported her from being "buyer" to being the "goods." Switching roles is a common way of dealing with your anxiety. You may, for instance, be anxious about being rejected and "switch" to overconfidence. You may worry about becoming sexually exploited and become emasculating instead. You may worry about feeling intimidated and become brash. Switching those from anxiety-charged roles is a way of trying to regain a sense of control.

Clearly, at that moment of deepest anxiety all sense of emotional independence is lost. Your self-definition becomes instantaneously determined by your interaction with your "prospect." If this is a repetitive problem for you, it may be difficult, if not impossible, to immediately change this behavior, because your responses have become ingrained and automatic. But you can retrain your mind by spending time in less anxiety-charged settings in which you practice being in the company of potential romantic interests.

A good way to work through your self-consciousness in coed social situations is to organize some sort of group yourself that allows you to meet others but in a socially diluted setting. For example, you might host a party for a friend and extend your guest list to include people you might be interested in. You might start a club organized around a favorite activity—skiing, softball, reading, gourmet cooking, or attending concerts—and ask friends to invite other guests regularly or occasionally. You might consider hosting an annual event, such as a tailgate party at a football game or a picnic at the Fourth of July fireworks. Hosting a group event catapults you into a psychological state of emotional independence because you're required to be a leader and to help others feel comfortable. You're restructuring your role to become someone who hosts, rather than hooks, your other.

It's ironic that the biggest challenge to maintaining emotional independence in the first phases of falling in love is idealization of your other, because disillusionment is the problem later on. Every once in a while one hears of a long marriage in which that idealization never dies, but it's rare; usually when you hear older people lavishly praise their spouses, it's after they've died. Too often, de-idealization leads to intense disappointment: What happened to the person I fell in love with? Unrealistic expectations on a spouse can lead to resentment and, later, detachment.

My patient Terry actually started her relationship with Dan with the same googly-eyed, goofy-love attraction that so unglued Ginnie when she met someone attractive. Within a few years of marriage, however, Terry and Dan had established a very different dynamic, for Terry spent much of her time frustrated and irritated with Dan. She longed to reestablish a sense of romance, but to do so would mean revising the way she negotiated conflict with Dan. Here's how she described a typical scene from their marriage.

Exiling Love: The Penal Colony

Terry drummed her acrylic nails rhythmically on the granite kitchen counter as she tried to watch the news. *Six forty-five and he's still not home. Why is it too much to ask him to remember our anniversary? Why am I always the one who has to plan every damn thing? If he really cared about us, wouldn't you think that just once . . .*

The garage door squeaked open and the engine of his Chevy rattled one last time as he turned off the ignition. *Why won't he get that thing tuned?* she thought. Dan came up the kitchen steps, walked over to her, and pecked her cheek, nearly missing her face as she turned to the side. *He clearly had no clue.* "Hi, sweetie!" he said.

"Hi."

"Whatsa matter?"

Silence.

"Okay, so are we going to play twenty questions?"

"You really did forget, didn't you."

He sat down next to her and thought. "Okay, let's think. October twentieth. Jeez, it's our anniversary. You're right, I did forget. You should have reminded me!"

"Why is it always my job to remind you? Why couldn't you just for once remember on your own?"

"You're right. I'm sorry. Look, let's not let it ruin the night. Let's go out for dinner. I'll take you anywhere you want."

"Dan, forget it. It's spoiled for me."

Whenever Dan disappointed Terry, she would load him up in

her psychological rowboat and take him off to the penal colony to serve his sentence. Once on the island—a barren, rocky place where the sun never shone—she would berate him. Sometimes it was a real-life dressing down, though the verbal exchanges were usually rather brief. What really consumed her time was the hours she would spend mentally chastising her husband for his transgressions. Of course, the experience was far more punitive for her than it was for Dan, for he would usually shrug off the episode rather quickly.

Terry's penal colony was a mind state in which she was unable to feel love, much less express it. Curiously, she actually had a desperate wish to be loved, coupled with deep anxiety about being rejected or neglected. The strength of those emotions made her terribly sensitive to hurt. At the slightest whiff of rejection, she would make a preemptive strike, as if deep in her unconscious mind she was thinking, "Hah! He won't catch me off guard this time! I'll reject him before he can reject me!"

Terry had erected two mental images of her husband. Either Dan would be the doting husband who would remember the anniversary as a sign of his love for her, or he would become the inconsiderate dolt who ignored her year after year. Yet in so doing, she also assigned herself corresponding roles: she would be either the adored, privileged wife receiving her husband's attention or the victimized, angry shrew holding Dan hostage with her anger. Neither set of images left room for her husband to be a fairly typical, well-meaning, but forgetful husband who could rise to the occasion of an anniversary with a bit of prodding. Therefore, she couldn't be the emotionally independent, well-loved woman who would have fun even if she had to make the restaurant reservations. Terry's excursions to the penal colony frequently prevented her from experiencing love. Ironically, love was what she craved the most.

A few days later, we talked about the episode.

"It's always like this. Everything is always up to me. Who has to remember the anniversary? Me. Who has to make the reservations? Me. Who is the one to call our friends and see if they want to join us? Me. I'm sick of it."

"But, Terry, it's not quite fair to say that it's all up to you. After all, at the end of the evening when the waiter brings the check, it is Dan's earnings that pay for it. Isn't that a contribution?"

"Oh, I don't know, I think he works because he likes it. Sometimes I think he'd rather be at work than at home. I just get tired of feeling like his mom. The way I feel about the anniversary was, like, if he can't even remember the date, then what's the point? How much does he really care?"

"On what rock is it carved that remembering an anniversary is the proof of love? Maybe that's your proof. But maybe his proof is something different. Maybe for him providing a life of comfort for you is how he shows his love. Maybe trying to cheer you up when you're mad at him, or sticking by you when you're feeling premenstrual, is his proof of love."

"Well, I suppose so. I just wish that once in a while he would do something romantic, just anything that would make me feel special."

Of course Terry wanted to feel special; what could be easier to understand? The problem was that she and Dan were like the Frenchman and the Englishman who were bickering over a sale. The Frenchman kept offering francs, and the Englishman only wanted pounds. Each felt he was being perfectly fair and generous in the trade, but neither was able to value the other's currency. Terry and Dan traded in different emotional currencies, and they could not understand why their respective offerings were unappreciated.

I suggested to Terry that she work on staying within her emotional boundaries and not have her mood and behavior become so reactive to Dan's forgetfulness. Could she remember who Dan was as a total person, rather than focusing exclusively on his lapse of memory? If Terry could learn how to talk with Dan without putting him on the defensive, perhaps he could learn how to deal in her currency. But to do that, she would have to redefine his forgetfulness. Maybe she'd have to understand it as just a human flaw.

Part of the problem with Terry's focus on Dan's forgetfulness was that it actually made him behave worse, not better. As a rule of thumb, our minds will tend to take our innate temperament and traits and use them as an all-purpose response to conflict. Dan tended to be forgetful anyway; he had had ADHD as a child. The more Terry berated him, the more anxious he became around her, which only made his absentmindedness worse. If Terry could only lighten up, the whole cycle might improve.

I wish I could report that after making this suggestion to Terry, she came to the next session saying, "Gee, Dr. Austin, after that really insightful comment you made, everything in my life suddenly changed! My marriage has improved dramatically!" In fact, Terry and I worked on this issue over and over for months before she began to have insight into herself. As she gained insight, she was able to feel more empathy for Dan.

More on Empathy

Empathy, which is such a useful skill when you are trying to evaluate your other, is also able to douse your emotional fires when you're about to overreact. Remember, empathy is the ability to get "in the skin" of another person, to accurately imagine what he or she must be thinking or feeling at a given moment. Imagine, for instance, if Terry could have paused long enough to have true empathy for Dan. She might have been concerned about how stressful his daily work life was, and how unselfish it was that he worked so hard. She might have imagined what it felt like for him to be absentminded, to kick himself for forgetting something as important as their anniversary. She might also have considered what it felt like to be on the receiving end of her wrath.

The pause for empathy blocks your activation of maladaptive templates. It becomes far more difficult to automatically ascribe a role to your other once you begin to try to understand his or her experience of the moment. Empathy blocks self-absorption, for your focus is on another human being. As you lift yourself out of the role of victim, you automatically return to your safety zone. Perhaps empathy could have allowed Terry to have a delightful, romantic anniversary with Dan.

The Biggest Challenge to Empathy: Anger

Among the emotions most destructive to your ability to get the love you want are harshness and anger. Anger is an important emotion, your warning signal that sounds when your needs and rights are being infringed. It's often triggered by unconscious anxiety. Anger, however, absolutely blocks your capacity to be empathic to the feelings of others as much as empathy diminishes anger.

I've never met a person who truly wanted to be angry, and all of us know what it is to struggle to forgive and let go of irritation, hostility, or even rage. The single best way to let go of anger is to step into someone else's skin and observe yourself through his or her eyes.

I experienced that some time ago and it helped me with my anger in one particular setting. Like anyone who travels by air, I've had my share of lost baggage. The first few times that happened, I expressed my frustration to the lost-baggage clerk. Then one time I had to stand in the baggage office and watch the clerk interact with a long line of irritated, tired travelers. One after another, they expressed their frustration, just as I had. I watched their faces and saw every variation of anger, ranging from indignation to outrage. And I watched the clerk handle each customer with self-control and professionalism. But I could also see the clerk shut down emotionally. I could only imagine what if feels like to get up each morning and look forward to another long line of angry people.

That did it for me. Now I'm always nice to lost-baggage clerks. I've learned to always travel with a change of undies and my makeup bag with me.

So if you're having trouble letting go of anger and remaining empathic to your other, try to watch him for a while as he struggles with the issues of his life. Look for those moments when you can admire his courage, applaud his resourcefulness, or appreciate his good humor. And remember that the healing of anger is never straightforward, but surges and recedes like the ocean as the tide goes out in waves.

Passive Aggression

Anger in close relationships is most often expressed as passive aggression, for it is far easier to express your frustration through sins of omission than by active conflict. Commonly we think of passive aggression as the expression of anger by withholding or frustrating behavior. In my clinical work, however, I've found it more helpful to think of it as the enormous range of behaviors one observes in individuals who are both passive and quite angry. And since even the most assertive people are frequently passive in some aspects of their relationships, passive aggression is extremely common.

Anger is such an uncomfortable emotion that we often try to hide it from others. The way you disguise your anger may even be so clever that you fool yourself. You behave in ways that punish or frustrate others while being consciously unaware of the depth of your feelings. Victoria struggled with this problem and came to see me for what she hoped would be a few counseling sessions. She and Angelo were a little further along in their marriage than Terry and Dan and were struggling over delegating home responsibilities and child-rearing.

"It's my marriage," she told me, looking at me through long black bangs. "It's just not working and I'm starting to feel like I made the biggest mistake of my life. Somehow I've managed to get myself into the worst of a traditional marriage and the worst of a modern marriage.

"Angelo and I have been married for eight years. We have one child, who is six. Both of us work—I'm a schoolteacher. And we both come from pretty traditional Hispanic homes, and he still has this macho thing going on deep inside him, I just know he does, even though he would deny it. He'd say, 'Well, sweetie, I've never held you back from what you wanted to do. I let you go to work—isn't that what you women-libbers want?' I could kill him when he says that, it just makes me so mad. He's so clueless about what he's saying. 'I *let* you work?' Puh-lease!

"The thing that gets me crazy is that he does *nothing* around the house. Like with our son—he'll do the fun stuff, like take him to a baseball game. But when it comes to things like making him brush his teeth, straighten his room, or helping him with his reading, he just doesn't want to be bothered.

"So here's a typical scenario. I leave school in the afternoon and go pick up little Angelo. We go home, and I try to get him settled down with the computer or something while I grade papers. When that's done, I start getting dinner ready. Big Angelo comes home late and so we eat late. Then after dinner he goes and watches TV while I clean the kitchen. Then after that I do the laundry and pick up the house. By now he's usually zonked on the sofa. I'll be like, 'Angelo, can't you be part of the family,' and he's like, 'I know, honey, I'm just too tired tonight.' Then finally I get done with my housework and he staggers off to bed. On weekends it's the same, except that I'm usually running errands all day or trying just to get ready to start another week. I'm like this super-mom. I try to be a good wife, work, take care of our son and the house, but it's just grinding me down."

What a baby Angelo is! I think. Victoria works so hard, and here he is, perpetual child, acting like she's his mom. Then I catch myself. Hold on, Linda. It's easy to get sucked in by hearing just one side of the story. There's always another side. We'd better do some couples counseling. Wonder what Angelo's version is?

A week later Angelo came in with Victoria. To my surprise, I liked him immediately. I had expected him to be somewhat arrogant and inflexible, based on Victoria's description. But he greeted me warmly and talked readily.

"We've got to do something," he said. "I just can't stand it anymore. We're in debt up to our eyeballs, and it seems like the more I work, the more Victoria spends. Yeah, I know she works, too. But she spends more than she makes, and she spends it on all this stuff we really don't need. Like last weekend it was a pair of new lamps that cost three hundred dollars each. For her the house has to be perfect, and each thing she buys has to be just the right thing. It feels like there's no getting ahead. The last time I got a really big promotion was a few years ago, and immediately she insisted we needed to move to a bigger house. The new mortgage was bigger than my raise had been, so we were in worse financial shape than before.

"I work as a salesman at a car dealership, and I'm, like, the highest producer there. But I'll tell you, it's really stressful work. You have to deal with these people all day long who come in, and sometimes they just want to joyride around in your cars for a few hours. Then you'll get one who you think is going to buy something, and at the last minute they tell you that they're going to check things out on the Web and see if they can get a better deal.

"So then I come home, and the first thing I do is to check the mail. Half the time there's a credit card statement, or a new bill for the latest thing Vic thought she couldn't do without. But I'm so worn-out from the day I don't even have the energy to talk to her about it. So I just go and watch a game or something, have a beer or two, and try to just have a little peace and quiet before the next day starts."

Victoria and Angelo had what might be called a neotraditional marriage, not uncommon in contemporary society. They thought they were progressive in their views of gender roles, but they actually exploited each other. Angelo took advantage of Victoria by "letting" her work, while contributing little to the second shift at home. Victoria prided herself on having a career, but was irresponsible about sticking to a reasonable budget.

Together they created an interaction we eventually started calling Lord Knows I Tried. Lord knows Victoria tried to Do It All, and she genuinely thought she was doing everything she could possibly do to contribute to the family. Lord knows Angelo also tried to contribute by working as intensely and steadily as he could. However, both turned a blind eye to the kind of contribution their spouse needed and wanted. Angelo desperately needed Victoria to grow up and contribute by becoming financially responsible. Victoria desperately needed Angelo to grow up and contribute as a father and a participant in managing the home.

The two shared several common psychological patterns:

- Each of them played the role of martyr. Both believed they gave way more than 50 percent of their share to the family but were unappreciated for their efforts.

- Both of them knew their behavior enraged the other and yet turned a blind eye to the impact this had on the marriage.

- Each of them expressed anger passively by not doing what the other needed.

The essence of passive aggression is to express anger by not doing something. Almost always the passive aggressor denies that there's any connection whatever between the anger and the lack of contribution. Passive aggressive people are consciously unaware of their own hostility. In relationships in which both partners are passive aggressive, the pattern becomes more intense over time: Okay, buster, if you don't do X, I won't do Y.

Common passive-aggressive behaviors include:
Chronic lateness: Your tardiness communicates a clear message: My time is more valuable than yours. It's therefore more important that I squeeze in one more task before I see you than for you to waste your time waiting for me.

Forgetting commitments: It will always feel to you as if you "simply forgot." Invariably you forget things that you'd actually rather not do, but don't make an active decision to decline.

Making jokes at the other's expense: "Digs" are really a way of expressing hostility but denying your anger under the guise "I was only kidding." If you really want to alienate your other, just add, "Oh, you take yourself so seriously." There's really nothing funny about hurting someone's feelings.

Sloppiness: If your sloppiness affects your other's living space, or if it means that you lose or damage other people's belongings, you are expressing disrespect with your bad habits.

Annoying habits: You know you're really bugging the other person, but you persist anyway.

Hypochondriasis: If you complain a lot about aches and pains, you're probably a master's level passive aggressor. Constant complaints about body aches and pains is a way of stealing attention from others, and you're probably avoiding activities and responsibilities as well. It's passive because you're not dealing with issues directly and it's aggressive because you're getting on everyone's nerves.

Chronically needing to borrow money: If you're continually taking money from others and not paying it back, it's really not much different from stealing, except that your other can't prosecute you—much as they'd like to.

Not sharing work equally: Rather than taking someone's money, you're depleting them of relaxation time that they would undoubtedly would enjoy as much as you.

Expecting others to pick up the pieces of mistakes: It's understandable that it's a pain for you to have to fix your own mistakes. So why would you think someone else would want to do it for you?

Allowing others to make mistakes that could easily have been avoided: This occurs commonly in the business world, particularly in bureaucracies where being helpful often isn't rewarded. If you watch others struggle with problems that you could easily help them with, you're passively acting out your hostility.

Setting others up to look foolish: Just watch reality television and you'll realize that human beings enjoy watching other people look idiotic. If you get a kick out of watching someone else be embarrassed, you're passive aggressive.

Do you recognize yourself as passive aggressive? Almost all of us are from time to time, for it's an easy way to avoid direct conflict.

The "Who me, mad?" stance allows you the great pleasure of see-ing yourself as a benign, kindly person, while you still get to really stick it to the other guy. Like someone who's fallen in quicksand, you try to lie still on the surface of your anger out of fear of drowning in your wrath; yet you're equally unable to extricate yourself from the sticky mush of your emotions. Your "self" is noble, long-suffering, and martyred; your other is an insensitive jerk who doesn't appreciate you; and your mood is smoldering re-sentment that is denied or minimized. It's clever in its self-deception, and destructive to your love relationships.

To pull yourself out of the quicksand, here's a technique I've modified from Everett Worthington's fine book *Five Steps to For-giveness*. Force yourself to sit down and write a letter as if you were the person you've been difficult toward. Put yourself in his shoes, and force yourself to describe your behavior as he might. Write down the ways your lack of contribution affects the rela-tionship. Describe the feelings of resentment and hopelessness your passive behavior stirs up. Be as honest as you can as you write.

To relinquish passive aggression, work to become consciously aware of your behavior. Ask several people close to you if you have behavioral habits that irritate them, and listen carefully to their answers. The second step is to discipline yourself to turn passivity to contribution, resentment into responsibility. It's not an easy transition to make, but is so important in cleaning up your rela-tionships.

Midlife Envy

Envy, of course, is an emotion for all seasons and all ages, but is often enough a significant issue at midlife. In early adulthood, life is still filled with endless possibility. You may not be wealthy now, but who knows what lies ahead? Perhaps you've not found love yet, but who's in a rush? There's plenty of time. But by midlife one senses that options may be closing down. It's easy to look around and see others who have more money, more love, or smarter children than yours. It's easy to feel envious.

Of all emotions, envy is one of the most difficult and unpleasant to endure. It's the direct antithesis of emotional independence, for you're basing your concept of how you should live and what you should have on someone else's life. Envy acts like a strong acid, corroding your ability to love because you're prone to devalue the relationships you have. No one likes feeling envious, and most people recognize how destructive it is. Yet ridding one's emotional life of envy can be extremely difficult.

My patient Rebecca struggled with envy to an inordinate degree. She came in one day and threw herself down on my office sofa, looking drawn and unhappy as always.

"No one would believe what goes on inside me," she moaned. "To the outside world I'm just this really successful person. I have a husband that everyone thinks is the greatest guy, and I know he's about as good as they come. I have a little boy who's really bright and just a supersweet kid. My law practice is going incredibly. I just had a settlement on that big lawsuit I've been telling you about, and my split is over a million dollars. And of course there's that house we built that was supposed to have been our dream house.

"But none of it makes me happy, none of it. No matter where I go, no matter what I do, I feel envious of others. Like right now I'm sitting here thinking, 'I like your suit better than mine, I should never have gotten this color.' Where do you shop, by the way? Never mind, I know that's not the point. That's just an example of how I think, constantly. Last night my husband and I went out for dinner, and the whole time I was really pissed off because his food was better than mine. And then we ordered dessert, and I knew when the waiter left I'd made the wrong decision, so I made my husband trade with me.

"Making decisions is the hardest thing in the world for me. It almost killed me to build our house because there were so many things I had to decide. And every decision, I'd be thinking, 'What will people think if I get the doorbell that goes *dong-dong-ding* instead of plain old *ding-dong?* What will people think if I get a sisal rug instead of an Oriental?'

"The worst thing is that I know how incredibly stupid all this is. I know there are people out there who couldn't afford one room of my house, much less the whole thing, and I know I should be grateful that we're all healthy, knock on wood. I know how ridiculous all this is, but it doesn't help me to stop.

"My whole life is absolutely consumed by regrets. Like right now I'm really worried about our son because his grades aren't very good. I think he's ADD. My husband's nephews are ADD and I think he got it from his side of the family. I really should have married someone else. And I really hate all the social stuff I have to do for his work. It all gets me down just to see all those other women who have better clothes, better husbands, smarter kids. I just feel so depressed all the time."

Rebecca was, without a doubt, the most envy-driven person imaginable, and the depth of her feelings was all the more unfathomable because she lived a life of material excess. Her story is worth telling because it illustrates one of the great ironies of human nature: the feeling of envy has nothing to do with what you do have, and everything to do with your perception of what you don't have. And since no human being, not even Bill Gates, owns everything, it's always possible to feel consumed by envy. In fact, many of the most materially endowed people are the most envious, for their material accumulation is driven by envy to begin with. One man explained it to me this way: "The best way I know of to keep from being envious of others is to make them envious of me."

For some people envy is so dominant that it exudes a pea green smog that covers their personalities; that was the case for Rebecca, who had a narcissistic personality disorder. She experienced her self as chronically deprived of what she wanted but entitled to more, while others were seen as unfairly privileged. Severe envy is indeed characteristic of narcissistic people, for their psychology is based on an inflated, though brittle, image of themselves that makes them feel entitled to all that they see. When they are not sufficiently catered to by life, their self-esteem crumbles. For most people, envy does not become a world unto itself, but even small islets create fumes that contaminate your emotional environment. When you feel envious, your self is impoverished, defeated, or deprived, and others are unfairly fortunate, rewarded, or indulged. Your state of mind is colored by resentment and self-pity. As happened to Rebecca, when envy becomes pervasive and consuming, it may lead to depression. And depression, the state of ultimate joylessness, is an epidemic in modern American society. Sophisticated epidemiologic research indicates that each decade of the past century has witnessed a significant increase in clinical depression, even though our level of material prosperity has risen in tandem.

Unfortunately, it appears that something about our culture makes us depressed in spite of—maybe because of—our great affluence. Researchers have documented that Caucasian Americans experience depression twice as frequently as Mexicans living in Mexico. The obvious question is whether this difference is due to genes or environment. However, second- or third-generation Mexican-Americans living in the United States experience rates of depression equal to Caucasian Americans. It is deeply ironic that immigrants come to our country to escape grinding poverty and to experience opportunity and prosperity. Yet something about contemporary American culture promotes emotional impoverishment.

The comparisons of Americans and Mexicans give powerful clues about which conditions allow joy and which promote its opposite, depression. All humans attempt to find joy by seeking prosperity and comfort. But happiness is clearly not dependent on your external environment. It's created by your internal environment, for the room where you live every minute of your life is within your mind. It doesn't matter at all how luxurious your surroundings are if your internal room is dark and dank.

A simple truth: we are happy when reality meets our expectations. You can observe this within yourself moment by moment. You could, for instance, cook yourself a simple meal and be quite satisfied with it. But if you were to go out to a good restaurant with the expectation of having a fine meal, you would become quite unhappy if you were served that same simple meal. I suspect that the native Mexicans are happy because their lives go pretty much as expected. When their children become acculturated to this country, they become just as miserable as your average red-blooded American, for they, too, are inundated with the messages of an envy-driven culture.

Any type of major loss increases the gap between expectation and reality. Deep attachments lead to the expectations of permanence, whether you're attached to a person, a job, a pet, or your home. When that expectation is shattered, your mind does not easily let go. You launch a clenched-fist-shaking-at-the-sky protest in which you are constantly comparing current reality with your expectations. The bigger the gap, the more depressed you become regardless of other blessings in your life.

Frank McCourt describes this dynamic and the devastation it

wreaks in his book *Angela's Ashes*. McCourt was one of eight boys born to an Irish family; his father was a severe alcoholic and a wastrel, and the family was constantly desperately poor. Due to poor nutrition and care, one of his younger brothers died. His mother became so distraught and depressed that she increasingly neglected the remaining boys. As a result, another little boy died. Again she became overwhelmed by her grief toward that son, neglecting her remaining sons even more—and so another one died. In all, she lost a total of four sons in this manner. The story of Angela is a parable for the human tendency to damage what we do have while we grieve over what we don't have.

I once saw a bumper sticker that read, "I feel so much better since I gave up all hope." There's tongue-in-cheek wisdom in those counterintuitive words. You can probably remember a time in your life when you beat your head against the wall, trying to fix a relationship or turn back the clock to undo a mistake. To whatever extent "giving up hope" means closing the gap between reality and expectations, you begin to feel happier.

Using Envy as a Stimulus to Personal Growth

Envy is composed of two parts. There is often an unhealthy part, based on unrealistic ideas about what you're jealous of. But there's also a healthy part of envy, for it can lead you to take steps to improve your life. To step out of envy and reground yourself in emotional independence so you can make positive changes, try the following:

1. Learn about the total life of the person you envy. Envy is almost always based on a partial understanding of another's life. You may envy another's material wealth, but

would you really want to be married to her husband or work the long hours she has to achieve it? If you're envious of your friend's marriage, would you really be willing to put up with his mother, the children of his first wife, or the demands of his work life?

2. Learn more about the lives of successful or happy people. Is your envy based on an immature idea that there are perfect people who live perfect lives? If you study the biographies of famous people, you will invariably learn of periods of great trauma or struggle in their lives. You'll realize that what you're envious of represents a tiny slice of time in their lives; the past was often far more difficult, and their future is unpredictable. Think of the example of Princess Diana, whose glamour, wealth, beauty, and fame surely stirred up envy at many points in her life. Yet her mother left her when she was six, her marriage was a disaster, and she died at thirty-six. Not much to envy there.

3. Ask yourself what you'd be willing to sacrifice to get what you're envious of. If you're envious of the career of your friend the lawyer, why not apply to law school? If you're envious of your friends with children, why not adopt one of the millions of children who needs a home? If you're envious of your sister's great figure, why not commit to a better diet and daily exercise? If you're envious of your coworker's latest promotion, why not put in longer hours at the office? Remind yourself that you have real choices about the life you create for yourself.

4. Find the healthy part of your envy and transform it into inspiration. Many of the really good goals we set for

ourselves are inspired by the examples of others. Maybe you envy something you see that really would improve your life. Use your envy to fuel your determination to make positive choices in your life.

5. And last but by no means least, commit yourself to spiritual growth based on a deeper understanding of what's really important in life. Remind yourself that being a good person doesn't automatically entitle you to good fortune, nor does your friend's good fortune mean that she's a better person than you. If life actually worked that way, given what a large fraction of the world's population lives in desperate poverty, you might well have far less than you do—I'm sure I would. Work to develop a deeper sense of appreciation for all you have.

Polarized Roles in Long Marriages

I have an uncle who wears a hearing aid. His wife, whom he loves dearly, could nonetheless be fairly said to talk too much and too loud. So Unkie solves the problem easily: the louder she talks, the lower down he turns his hearing aid. So she shouts more, and he turns the volume lower.

So it goes in long relationships. Interlocking patterns of behavior develop in which each partner becomes more extreme. Each excess triggers an escalated reaction. Roles are polarized, and in time the relationship becomes a parody. I'll see you and raise you.

You may have grown up laughing at the marital aikido of Edith and Archie or Lucy and Ricky Ricardo, but in real life it's not that funny. The marriage of Sandy and Chris is an example of how exaggerated marital roles can become, and how destructive to self-esteem that process is. Highlights from their marital therapy:

SANDY: You're always so quiet. I wish you'd just talk more. Share your feelings. Look at me, I always share my feelings. You always know what I think, right? You may not like it, but at least you know. You, on the other hand, just clam up. I really wish I knew what was going on inside you.

CHRIS: I'd like to talk more, but I just don't know what to say sometimes. Sometimes I try, but it seems like you—

SANDY: Don't listen? What do you mean, I don't listen? I listen. I really try hard to get you to open up. Why is it my fault? It seems like everything is always my fault. You always criticize me. I really try hard to be a good partner. I do so much for you. Sometimes I think you just don't really like the real me. You don't see how hard I try.

Later . . .

CHRIS: I really wish I could help you feel better about yourself.

SANDY: I do feel good about myself. In fact, I feel great about myself. I've never felt better about myself.

CHRIS: Well, I know, but you've been talking about having another plastic surgery. It'll be the third operation, now. It just seems like every few years—

SANDY: Look, I like to look good. I just don't want to look like all those wrinkled, tired-looking women I see around. You wouldn't like me that way either. That's part of me, to look good. Why can't you just accept that

about me? Why can't you just love me the way I am?
(Tears up.) You just want me to be one of those Birken-
stock granola-crunchers. Well, that's just not who I am!

And a bit later:

CHRIS: I know I'm not very outgoing. I'm just not that
comfortable around large groups of people.

SANDY: Me, I'm just the opposite. I've always wished I
could be onstage, I think it's really fun. I never saw a
microphone I didn't love. And I love being with people,
going to parties. I just always feel, if I can just get you
used to going, you'll learn to like it. You don't even have
to say much when we go, you can just stand with me
and I'll do the talking. But I think it's really important
for us just not to sit home all the time.

CHRIS: That's not really that much fun for me, to be honest, to stand there like a bump on a pickle.

SANDY: So then try harder! Talk, already! Just watch how I
do it.

Okay, I exaggerated this conversation just a teeny little bit, but
honestly, not that much. Over time, Sandy and Chris had become
caricatures of themselves. The quieter Chris was, the more uncomfortable Sandy became, and the more she talked to fill the
void. But then, as she increasingly sensed his tension, she became
scared of what she'd hear if he did start talking: Who knew what
he might say? So she would preemptively finish his sentences,
then launch into an impassioned defense of herself that sounded
more like the closing argument of a trial than a thoughtful conversation.

Hush, Sandy, I would think as she rattled on. Be still. Let Chris just talk. Let him be the one to break the silence. Make it safer for him to say what he feels. Don't punish him with guilt for daring to say what's on his mind.

As Chris had become increasingly withdrawn from Sandy, her self-esteem had begun to falter. She had one, then two plastic surgeries and was now contemplating a third. Would this rekindle his love for her? The thought that Chris didn't find her attractive was devastating, and she responded with a tidal wave of pseudo-confidence.

Sandy, slow down. Stop protesting so much. Within every person who proclaims her excellent self-esteem is someone who feels really, really fragile. How can Chris ever feel safe really expressing himself if he's just knocked back with a barrage of your bravado?

And as time wore on, Sandy became increasingly competitive with Chris. She prided herself on her extroversion and social skills and dominated interactions with other couples. This, of course, made Chris acutely uncomfortable and he withdrew even further.

Sandy and Chris each erected complementary templates in reaction to each other. In response to Chris's aloofness, Sandy's mental image of her self became assertive, outgoing, and charming—causing her behavior to become domineering, superficial, and manipulative. Her other—that is, her mental image of Chris—became someone who was boring, cold, and withdrawn. The emotional coloration she brought to her template varied; what she tried to feel was self-confident and vivacious. Her template, of course, was brittle, as evidenced by her easy tearfulness; at those times her self became a sad little girl trying to please, her other was rejecting and withholding, and the emotional coloration was depression.

Chris erected a template of his own. Quiet and introspective by nature, as he became irritated by Sandy, his self became moody and withdrawn, while his other—his mental image of Sandy—was someone vain, superficial, and socially insensitive; and the emotional coloration was despair.

Penetrating psychological insight was not Sandy's forte, so I gave her some concrete rules, which amounted to trying to dislodge her template to put her back in emotional independence:

1. If you really want Chris to speak, be quiet and listen.

2. If you want Chris to enjoy social gatherings, stand by his side and let him take the lead.

3. If you want to know what Chris feels about you, don't become defensive when he opens up. Just be interested.

4. Try to spend as much time listening to your inner voice as you spend talking to others.

5. If you really want plastic surgery, get plastic surgery. But do it for your own sake, not because you think Chris will lose interest in you otherwise.

And Chris got some concrete suggestions:

1. Don't withhold compliments from Sandy just because you know she's fishing for them.

2. If you're going to show up at social events, really show up. Try to engage. It makes everyone feel awkward if you act as if you'd rather not be there.

3. If you don't want to go to an event, say so clearly. Propose an activity you would enjoy more and ask Sandy to join you.

4. If Sandy interrupts you, tell her to be quiet and let you finish. Don't just clam up.

Sandy's behavior dictated Chris's behavior and vice versa. Each activated each other's worst templates. The challenge was to unhinge them from each other, so each could reclaim emotional independence rather than knee-jerk reactivity.

When I was a child, parents would have birthday parties for their kids without hiring clowns and ponies. Instead they would make us play fun games such as the three-legged race. We kids would line up in pairs, and one leg of each child would be tied to the other child's. The pairs were supposed to race up the field, but mostly we would fall over in little piles, and everyone would think it was funny.

Marriage can be like a three-legged race. You tie yourselves together, then see how far you get. When you fall down, however, it's not that funny. Usually it would all go much better if you untied the rope and just walked along together, close but separate.

The stories I've told illustrate only some of the potentially infinite number of potential templates of interaction that block love. Your own templates are unique to you. No one else has your exact personality. Your templates reflect reenactments of relationships you had with important people in your past, particularly parents and other family members. You re-create your childhood relationships by foisting on others the dramas you experienced growing up. You define the role of your other based on how you experienced others in your past, reliving the roles you played in your original family.

Alternatively, you may reverse those ancient roles. Your self may become a caricature of an important someone in your past, and your other becomes the you of your childhood. A familiar example of this role reversal is the abused boy who grows up to become a wife beater; he says, in fact, "I will no longer be the terrified, overwhelmed little boy cowering in the corner. Now I will be the big, strong, angry one, and my wife will be the small, helpless victim. That way, I'll never have to be scared again."

Reenactments of the past are by no means always negative. The best parts of your personality reflect reenactments of loving, happy experiences in your life. Your capacity to experience love was developed as you engaged with your original family and observed them loving you and others.

Most of us grew up in homes that provided a mixture of relationships and experiences. We had parents and siblings who were neither all-good nor all-bad, but had templates of their own that emerged in daily life. The rich, unique, and multicolored nature of your own personality reflects the emotional complexity of your past. Your challenge, of course, is to learn to sift through that complexity and activate the healthiest parts of your emotional life. A simple, but challenging "rule" will help you stay oriented to that task: to stay emotionally independent, relinquish trying to control the emotions and behavior of other people.

Activating unhealthy templates almost always begins with your attempts to manage or manipulate the behavior of others. At times, you may try to do this directly by offering advice or even becoming angry. At other times, you may observe yourself expecting others to read your mind and discern your wishes. Terry's trip to the penal colony, for instance, was precipitated by her efforts to control Dan's behavior around the events of their anniversary, while Victoria's passive aggression was triggered by her efforts to control Angelo. The more you can allow others to feel what they feel and behave as they wish, the more emotional room you will have to experience love.

Learning to stay emotionally independent is a gradual process, not an all-or-none phenomenon. Begin by setting modest goals for yourself. You can try not to ask intrusive questions about the private affairs of others. You can remind yourself that your friends and family have the right to manage their own relationships with others. You can make plans to pursue your own goals rather than to control others' lives. Even making a little progress in staying within the boundaries of your own life will allow you to experience love more richly.

As you focus your energy on managing your own behavior, it will help you to concentrate on living fully in the here and now. The past is over and you can't change it. The future may never come, so you can't change that by worrying about it. You can, however, take control of now—what you are able to accomplish yourself. Remind yourself that if it is hard enough to control your own feelings and behavior, your chances of controlling others' is slim indeed

Strategies for Establishing Emotional Independence

Predict and Avoid

In time, you'll be able to easily predict the situations that are prone to catapulting you into enmeshed, reactive interactions. There's absolutely nothing wrong with avoiding tough situations altogether. No, you don't need to worry that you'll be sweeping problems under the carpet. (What else are carpets for?) Really significant problems will always scamper out from under the rug sooner or later. For now, you're tending to your own emotional health and development, and taking the steps you need to experience the life you want to create for yourself.

For Terry, for instance, could predict that Dan would forget every birthday and anniversary and that she would be incited to row out to the penal colony. Could anything really be gained by proving Dan's forgetfulness one more time? Why not just remind Dan ahead of time that an anniversary was approaching? The solution to Terry's problem—reminding Dan—is so obvious that there must be a psychological reason that Terry resisted this. In fact, the periodic skirmishes allowed Terry to maintain the upper hand in the relationship and gave her a feeling of moral superiority over Dan. The challenge for Terry was to resolve her issues about their power imbalance—and to avoid the penal colony twice a year by simply reminding Dan of the dates.

The predict-and-avoid strategy can be used to circumvent an enormous array of problems. Perhaps your sister-in-law drinks too much at dinner and has been resistant to your suggestions that she talk to a counselor about her substance abuse. Instead of repeating the same inebriated scenario, invite her instead to go out for an afternoon of shopping or a walk on the beach, sites where she is unable to begin to drink. Perhaps you invariably argue with your husband about the way he behaves at your parents' house. Plan instead to visit them by yourself. Or maybe your arguments are triggered by your husband's going out on Fridays for a beer after work. Find a time each week for an independent activity that you'd enjoy—a movie date with a girlfriend or a class you'd like to take. What each of these situations has in common is refusing to experience yourself as aggrieved and victimized and finding a place where you can meet your emotional needs on your terms.

Buffer Your Difficult Relationships

As you begin to examine your alter personality islands, you will observe templates that frequently get activated with particular individuals. Perhaps you never become passive aggressive—except with your boss. Maybe you never become a martyr—except with your mother. And maybe a friend or two regularly cause you to set sail for the penal colony.

Obviously, the easiest solution here is to let go of the relationship altogether. But perhaps it's not so easy to quit your job. Hopefully you realize that you'd rather heal your relationship with your mother rather than never see her. Maybe you recognize that the friend who irritates you has other wonderful traits.

In chemistry, a buffer is a substance that acts to keep the acidity of a solution in a desired range. Likewise, you can think of strategies that will neutralize the intensity of your interactions. Perhaps you do better with your mother if your sister is around, or maybe you need to go out with your friend Jennifer only in groups. Alternatively, you may observe that certain painful interactions occur only when a third party is around; maybe you and your mother get along fine except when your sister is around. The point is to observe the dynamics and details of what repetitively makes a relationship problematic, and to try to avoid problematic configurations of people.

Impose Time Limits on Stressful Situations

The saying "Fish and houseguests begin to smell after three days" reflects that the stress of playing host begins to build after several days. In fact, any stressful situation takes an increasing toll over time. You may have observed particular settings in which you are able to remain emotionally independent but for so long before a deterioration phase begins.

Susan habitually hosted Christmas Day festivities for her extended family. The tradition was that everyone would arrive at her home by 9 A.M. and the children would exchange their gifts. By 10 A.M. the children would be racing around the house, beating each other over the head with various blunt instruments that Santa had brought. Parents would begin yelling, and the holiday would be in full swing. By eleven the women would start cooking, and by noon they would be mad at all the men for not watching the children. By 1 P.M. two uncles would have started drinking heavily. Dinner would be served at three, and by three-fifteen the first glass of milk would have been spilled. By three-thirty, at least one inebriated uncle would have choked on his turkey and been thumped dramatically on the back; the episode would at least allow one member to act out his aggression. By 4 P.M. the men would have started arguing about politics. The children would be laughing hysterically, wailing miserably, and emitting ear-piercing shrieks in quick succession. By five the two uncles would mercifully be asleep in front of the tube. By six, cleanup would begin, and everyone would leave at seven-thirty.

It is exceptionally rare for any large family not to have a background of ancient conflicts, jealousies, and irritations, and Susan's family was no exception. Christmas Day had never progressed peaceably, not once. While Susan gained attention as the family martyr for hosting the event, she realized she had basically come to hate Christmas.

The solution she found was quite simple: invite people to come at four, serve dinner (potluck) by five, have dessert and gifts by six, and encourage the end of festivities by seven-thirty when the children were starting to whine. She also used heavy paper plates and plastic utensils to abort an extended cleanup and enlisted the aid of her older sister in keeping the event on schedule. Susan decided to serve no cocktails and only bought enough wine to refill glasses once. As a result everyone stayed reasonably sober, and much happier, throughout the event. When she polled her sister and sisters-in-law about how they liked the shorter day, each intimated they were delighted but hadn't suggested it earlier for fear of hurting Susan's feelings! She developed a new rule for determining the duration of Forced Family Fun: take the amount of time relatives ought to be reasonably expected to get along, divide by two, subtract an hour, and allow only that much time for the get-together.

In-law conflicts are a potent source of misery in a marriage. The amount of time you might naturally want to spend with your own parents, siblings, or children from a previous marriage is usually vastly more than your spouse would naturally want to commit. Start by accepting that simple difference as a normal, natural response, not something that either person has to feel guilty about. Stop pressuring your spouse to spend more time with your family than he or she wants. Make a reciprocal agreement that allows each of you time for extended visits with your own family if you desire, without the expectation that your spouse must accompany you.

Establish "Pots" of Money

Money is one of the most common issues that couples struggle over. It's hard to feel emotionally independent if you're financially broke. You can't free up a space in your heart to engage with your other if you're seething over his or her latest extravagance. As with Victoria and Angelo, resentment over financial issues spills over into other areas of your relationship, and a tit-for-tat cycle of getting even can make money issues spiral out of control.

Fortunately, simple banking practices can make it much easier to work these issues out. Here's what I suggested for Victoria and Angelo:

1. Set up an automatic deposit of your paychecks into your joint household account.

2. Establish three other accounts as well: Victoria's personal banking account; Angelo's personal banking account; and a savings/investment account.

3. Have the bank make automatic transfers of designated amounts each month into each of the three secondary accounts.

4. Tie personal credit cards to each separate account.

5. If you tend not to pay off your credit cards monthly, use debit cards instead. The frequent-flier miles or other benefits you may get from credit cards are not worth the cost of the interest on your unpaid balances.

Victoria and Angelo tried the system, and it worked. Victoria liked it because she could spend out of her pot without feeling guilty or defensive toward Angelo. Angelo liked it because he had the security of knowing that their savings/investment account was growing.

Establish "Pots" of Time

Just as Victoria and Angelo needed a system to given them each independent control over money, they needed a similar system for time. Here's what we came up with:

1. Designate specific "pots" of time as family time; Victoria and Angelo decided that dinnertime and until the children's bedtime would be family time that would be spent together. Friday nights would be designated family "party night" with popcorn and a video.

2. Designate specific "individual" time. After the kids' bedtime, Victoria and Angelo would each have an hour or so of free time for themselves. Further, Saturday afternoon would be Victoria's time to go shopping or meet friends for lunch; Sunday afternoon was Angelo's time to watch football or play tennis.

3. Designate time together. Victoria and Angelo decided to hire a baby-sitter on Saturday nights so they could go out to dinner or enjoy a movie.

Obviously the goal is not to become a slave to a schedule. But couples do set up de facto schedules anyway—one may always sack out on the sofa after dinner, while the other spends every evening on the phone, for example. Often, small modifications of those schedules can make a big difference in helping each person feel more content in the relationship. Victoria and Angelo observed their schedule more or less. The single biggest change they made, though, was that Angelo spent less evening time on the sofa and more time engaged with the family, and he felt that it was a good trade-off to have freedom on Sunday afternoons. Victoria felt much less resentful of Angelo's Sunday's watching TV football when she perceived it as a trade for her Saturday afternoons at the mall.

As you practice living within your boundaries, a wonderful, invisible process occurs: you mature. Your moods become gentler, you become kinder and more tolerant and less reactive to people and events. Most important of all, you become increasingly yourself. Living within your boundaries allows you to evolve into the life you want.

CHAPTER SIX

Evolve Consciously, Willfully, Healthily

LIFE REQUIRES US TO CHANGE AND GROW, and our personal evolution extends from cradle to grave. Our greatest emotional growth periods follow periods of great difficulty and challenge. To paraphrase Ernest Hemingway, life breaks all of us, and some grow stronger in the broken places. Without those break points, we would not be tested and challenged. We wouldn't grow stronger, and we wouldn't evolve.

While establishing emotional independence reflects relationship issues that are occurring today, evolution is a long-term process. Your preferred patterns of interaction developed over many years as you evolved in response to the human climate in which you lived. The way you develop in coming years will be influenced by your current relationships—or lack thereof!

Humans change and grow throughout their lives in different ways and for different reasons. Maturation, for example, is driven by the biological life cycle. Identification is the way you gradually become like people around you, taking on their habits and personality traits. But evolution results from the interesting and inventive ways you change in response to problems you encounter in your life and relationships.

Your evolution can be fast or slow, healthy or unhealthy. It may occur completely unconsciously, or you may choose to observe and direct it. If you have been holding yourself back from finding and keeping great relationships, it's time to take your evolution into your hand to become a person capable of great love.

Expanding Your Capacity to Evolve

Remember Chris and Sandy from the last chapter? Chris had originally come to see me for depression and marital problems. He had always been depressed, he said, and we were both over-joyed when he responded quickly to his antidepressant. But that helped only partially in improving his marital problems, and we decided to ask his wife to come in for couple's therapy. "I'd do al-most anything to try to make this marriage work," he said. "I just don't see divorce as a solution."

Sandy had a very different feeling, however. "Look," she said. "I am who I am. And I like who I am. And a lot of other people like me, too. I really don't want to change." I didn't know whether to be shocked by her rigidity and smugness or impressed that she was at least honest enough to admit what most people are unwill-ing to confess. Inner change is difficult, and most of us would do anything rather than take a hard look at ourselves, admit our shortcomings, and commit to do something about them. Even for Chris, making real change would not be easy.

Part of Sandy's resistance to self-examination reflected a basic personality style. She was not psychologically minded and prided herself on being practical rather than introspective. Part, also, was due to fragile self-esteem, for she became threatened and defen-sive when Chris or I suggested she look within herself. But a third part reflects that it's really hard for all of us to think about chang-ing. It means we have to admit that we're not perfect, that we don't have all the answers, and that others may have legitimate complaints.

Some years ago, I read an article by Andrew Tobias about financial investing that gave an important piece of advice. He noted that we tend to make our investment decisions today based on what we did in the past. "How can I sell my Lockheed stock at fifty when I bought it at fifty-five?" you think. The issue, Tobias says, is not what Lockheed did last week, last month, or last year. The issue is what you believe it will do in the future. Don't let your loyalty to your past investment decisions influence what your future decisions will be.

Similarly, Sandy was deeply invested in a personality style that had worked well for her in the past. She was so loyal to that style that she couldn't see that it wasn't working well for her in the present and was clearly going to cause her great trouble in the future if she couldn't change.

If you're single and you're interested in finding a great love, your need to evolve is especially important. Think back to your life five, ten, or fifteen years ago. Perhaps your single life worked well for you then. Is it still working for you? Perhaps the way you searched for relationships worked well then; is it still working for you? Perhaps the way you interacted in relationships worked well then. Is it still working for you?

Unlikely.

Whether you're married or single, the world around you is constantly changing. You must learn to change as well. Don't become a social dinosaur, able to thrive in one environment but doomed to extinction when conditions change.

Evolution, Revolution, and Stagnation

You can respond to the problems in your life in three fundamental ways:

- Evolution is your adaptation to specific problems in your unique interpersonal world. You can proactively guide your evolution by how you define those problems.

- Revolution is form of evolution in which you actively choose a different human environment. Whether your revolution is quiet or dramatic, it pushes you in new, life-altering directions. While to evolve is to attempt to fit in with your environment, to revolt is to seek a different environment.

- Stagnation occurs when you put yourself in a psychological holding pattern in your relationship, neither evolving nor revolting. Stagnation is emotional limbo. You go through the motions of living, but your will is paralyzed.

Evolution and revolution are essential activities in finding love. Without evolution you would be unable to respond to change. Without revolution, you would lose the opportunity to seize new opportunities and directions. It's important to maximize the power of each.

Evolution

You have evolved throughout your life to the conditions to which you have been exposed. Scientists have studied the genes-versus-environment question by looking at identical twins reared apart and have determined that between 30 and 50 percent of the factors that shape your personality reflect your adaptation to your human environment. You shape the world you live in, and that world shapes you.

At the times in your life when you are "broken"—or even just disappointed or frustrated—you must evolve to thrive again. When things are going well for you, you have no reason to change or challenge your thinking. Rather, it's when you've been knocked flat on your back that you're forced to stop to catch your breath. You consider your next move. Is it time for a change in posture or approach? Should your goals be reassessed?

The evolution of your heart, mind, and soul is not a steady, even process toward a well-defined goal. It's a back-and-forth journey: three steps forward, two back, seven steps forward, four back. The forward steps are important, of course, to make progress. But the backward steps are also important to give yourself a chance to change course if you need to. Because much of evolution is unconscious, the backward steps give you a chance to pause and take stock of the ways you've changed in response to recent experience. You can take some time to decide if you really like the direction you're going. Without consciously controlling your evolution, you face the danger of evolving in unhealthy directions.

Examples: Two women, Leila and Bertie, faced an all-too-common crisis in their late thirties: both were left by their husband without much warning. Both women were distraught about the experience, and both became significantly depressed for several months following the divorce. Leila eventually recovered from her depression and decided to work full-time. She became more involved in the lives of her teenage children as well as in some community projects. Her life became full and busy, but she shied away from romance. She gained weight and became self-conscious about her appearance. She sabotaged efforts by her friends to provide blind dates even though she said that she wanted to find someone; she would always seem to have a reason to reject a man before she even got to know him. She doubted her ability to make good choices about men and chose to live as a single woman. She had a full life in many ways, but even ten years later there was a wistfulness in her demeanor. She seemed neither sad nor truly happy.

Bertie had a quite different adaptation to her divorce. She moved to a large city where she thought she would have a better chance of finding a new relationship. She was, however, the opposite of Leila, not being discriminate in her choice of men. On two separate occasions, she became engaged and finally married a third man. The marriage was obviously a poor choice, and within a few years she chose to divorce.

The same problem, two very different paths of evolution in response, neither of them optimal. Both women had a severe crisis of self-confidence as a result of their divorce. Leila, however, seemed to see herself as unable to bear another disappointment and chose not to risk damaging her achy-breaky heart again. Bertie's behavior reflected the anguished question *Am I lovable?* Over and over she indeed found men to love her, but then dumped them, as if to say, "Now I will be the one to reject a man, rather than have a man reject me."

Neither woman made a conscious decision to pursue the particular path that she did, and neither would have predicted that she would end up alone a decade after her divorce. Yet in retrospect each could see how she had evolved.

At the time of crisis, it always seems as if the choices you are making are the most logical, sensible decisions, maybe the only decisions you can think of to make. Only when you look back can you appreciate how you've evolved.

Unless, that is, you make a willful decision to guide your evolution. Right now you are facing problems in your life that are shaping you. Since you're reading this book, you are probably struggling with a feeling that you are holding yourself back from love in some way, and you're interested in solving that problem. It's time to stop and look back at the path you've taken to get to this point.

So let's start with either your current relationship or the last one you were in if you are currently unattached. Your goal is to understand the impact that relationship had or is having on your personal evolution—positive, negative, or most likely, mixed. How has it affected your ability to love and be loved? Some questions to think about:

1. Why did you get involved with this particular person?

2. What issues from your past did you bring into this relationship?

3. What were you like when you entered this relationship? How emotionally grounded did you feel when the relationship started?

4. How have you changed since you've been in your most recent relationship?

5. What have been the best parts of this relationship, and how have they allowed you to grow?

6. What have been the problems with your lover, and how have you adapted to those problems?

7. What difficult parts of your personality has this relationship revealed to you?

8. What cherished parts of your personality have you abandoned?

9. How has your experience in this relationship affected your ability to find love in the future?

You may wish to go further back in your history, for you will be able to observe that each succeeding relationship answered some problem from the preceding one—and brought with it new problems. Bertie's path was, for instance:

First husband: An educated, cultured man who was emotionally withholding and eventually left her. Bertie married the sort of man her mother always wished she had married.

Fiancé 1: Bertie went into this relationship with the question *Can I be loved?* Her confidence was badly shaken by her divorce, and she had become rather insecure and needy. This man was significantly less educated than either Bertie or her first husband. He was, however, warm and affectionate, if somewhat impulsive and unreliable. It eventually became clear that he had a drinking problem and was flirtatious with other woman. Bertie became disgusted with his drinking and ended the relationship.

Fiancé 2: Bertie went into this relationship not only with remnants of *Can I be loved?* but with another question: *Can men be trusted?* After her divorce and first breakup, she had become cynical and mistrustful. This man was steady and reliable but was also a workaholic who usually spent what little free time he had with his children from his first marriage. Bertie initially liked him because he was much more responsible than Fiancé 1, but eventually came to resent his unavailability, and they ended the relationship after a series of arguments. Nonetheless, this relationship was stabilizing for Bertie. She did feel loved by this man, and she fundamentally trusted him. Her self-confidence was stronger at the end of this relationship than before it started.

Second husband: Bertie went into this relationship with the questions *Am I ever going to settle down again? Why do I keep jumping from man to man?* She had begun to lose faith in her ability to love deeply. This mind-set caused her to cast a blind eye to potential problems. This husband answered many of her previous questions. He was a good man, he loved her, he was committed, and he was faithful to her in the relationship. They dated for a year and then married. Fairly quickly, however, problems emerged. He was from a different country and had a different cultural background that made it hard for the two of them to empathically understand each other. He lost his job and was content to live off Bertie's salary; meanwhile, she lost her alimony when she remarried and felt financially pinched. She soon felt she had made a mistake and worried about becoming financially responsible for her new husband. She decided to bail out of the marriage.

Bertie's path illustrates some of the unhealthy ways people evolve after a traumatic breakup:

Overcorrection

Bertie responded to the way each previous man had behaved by overcorrecting on her next relationship, choosing men who had exaggerated versions of the traits she was seeking. She was so anxious, for example, not to choose a cold and unspontaneous man like her husband that she was overly attracted by her first fiancé's extroverted personality. She later overcorrected her growing difficulty with commitment by jumping into a marriage with the wrong person.

Overcorrection may take many forms. If your first spouse had problems with money management, you may find yourself drawn in your next relationship to someone who is overcontrolling of money. If you chose your first spouse because he or she came from a background similar to yours, you may choose your next spouse from a different ethnic group. Beware of overcorrections, for you may merely be trading in one set of problems for another.

Focusing on a single aspect of the relationship and ignoring other problems

Bertie's urgency to master an issue from a preceding relationship was so great that she ignored other obvious problems. Yes, she mastered issues the last relationship had brought her, but her emotional energy was so bound up in those old problems that she couldn't accurately predict new and different problems that were likely to arise.

If you have had a traumatic breakup, your attention will be focused on the issues that were painful in your old relationship. Be careful not to become blind to new issues that a new lover may bring.

Using a new relationship to restore your self-esteem

After a breakup, it's inevitable for your self-esteem to be damaged. You will tend to want to restore your self-esteem by finding someone to love you. You, like a ship with a hole in its hull, may find any harbor preferable to the open seas.

It's so human and common to want to use a new relationship to prove something to the lover who rejected you. The urge may be especially powerful if your old lover or spouse has moved on to a new relationship. *Look, someone loves me, too!* Resist the urge.

Becoming like the person who has hurt you

One of the ways that Bertie evolved following her first divorce was to become like her first husband, taking on the role of the dumper rather than the dumpee. In fact, it's common to imitate the traits of the one who has hurt you. You don't consciously think to yourself, "I'm going to turn into an SOB just like my lover." It's more subtle than that, ranging from a completely unconscious absorption of his or her traits to subliminal thoughts like "If he's going to be selfish, so am I. If he's going to be unfaithful, so will

I." You may be somewhat aware of a specific, concrete behavior you adopt, such as becoming unwilling to do housework because your spouse isn't pulling his fair share. What's harder to appreciate is when you co-opt a whole sector of your other's personality as a way of unloading the helplessness you have felt.

The tendency to avoid pain by identifying with the one who hurts you occurs in many marriages, as the case of Dora and Frank illustrates. Dora and Frank began to date in college, and when they began to talk of marriage, they spent hours spinning lovely visions of family life together. Dora supported the two of them through law school, working as a nurse. Frank was intensely driven and worked long hours; he was eventually chosen for law review. Once through law school, he clerked for a prestigious firm and subsequently became an associate. He became swept up in the quest for billable hours; when the Monday-morning tally of the previous week's productivity came out, he usually topped the list. Once he became a full partner, the complexity and visibility of his cases only increased.

In the early years of the marriage, Dora consoled herself over Frank's absence with the thought "When we just get through this period, it will change." She was right, it did change—it got worse year by year. Although she had always planned to have children, she was not able to get pregnant and began to take managerial courses in health administration. Eventually she got her master's degree, which led to a substantial increase in responsibilities. She stopped doing floor nursing and became a hospital administrator, working longer and longer hours.

Dora had spent years listening to Frank and his associates describe their hardball tactics in the courtroom. She herself became known in the hospital as a tough negotiator who alienated her associates because of her refusal to compromise. In her late thirties, though, her lifestyle began to catch up with her, for she developed migraine headaches that would keep her in bed for several days at a time. When her headaches failed to respond to treatment, she decided to come to therapy to ask, "Why is my body in revolt? Who have I become?"

Dora had never intended to become like Frank. For that matter, Frank hadn't really intended to become like the lawyers around him. But she had become just like Frank as a way of dealing with her disappointment with Frank.

Evolving to become like the lover who has hurt you "solves" a number of problems all at once. You don't have to feel like a victim anymore. You strengthen your tie to the one you have loved. You demonstrate your allegiance to his values. You boost your self-esteem by modeling yourself on someone you love. But the price you pay for this solution to your problem is high. After all, you can eventually get away from the one who has hurt you, but you can't get away from the self you have become.

A woman might evolve in numerous other ways in response to becoming single after a long relationship. Ideally, it would be wonderful to become more comfortable with sexuality, able to interact with a broad range of people, more self-confident—and tender and wise as a woman. To evolve in such positive directions would require great thoughtfulness about how one reacted to the crises, as well as purposeful, consciously controlled decisions about one's personal choices.

Evolution and Problem-Solving

In nature, all evolution occurs in response to a problem. Fir trees evolved in response to the "problem" of cold weather. Palm trees evolved in response to the "problem" of hot weather. Problems in nature are not necessarily good or bad, but they are stimuli that require change.

You, too, evolve when you are faced with a problem. Like a change in global climate, the problem may creep up upon you so gradually that you're not even aware of it. You begin to bend and change without realizing what you're doing. Over time you become a different person—for better or for worse.

Therefore, there is one overriding principle to observe: assume that anytime anything in your life changes, you are faced with the "problem" of adaptation. If your adaptation continues long enough, you will evolve. You don't have the choice whether or not to change, but you can choose whether you will observe and direct that change—conscious evolution. There are three steps to this process:

1. Consciously recognize your problem.

2. Define the problem in a way that allows you to do something about it.

3. Evolve in order to solve the problem.

Recognizing Your Problem

It's not at all uncommon to feel blindsided by a painful interpersonal problem, whether it's a sudden divorce, the end of a friendship, a child with a psychiatric problem, or losing your job. When that occurs, you feel a sense of shock and utter disbelief. How could such a thing happen to me?

Yet problems do not arise out of thin air. Typically, issues have been festering under the surface that have gone unnoticed and unaddressed. Sooner or later, any unresolved personality issue or emotional problem you have will trip you up. Others may have seen the problems coming for a long time. It's one of the many miracles of the unconscious that we can fool ourselves into thinking that everything is okay.

Dr. Randy Nesse, an evolutionary psychiatrist, has proposed a theory to explain the reason we trick ourselves. In all of nature, he says, animals wear camouflage to protect themselves from predators. Humans, living closely together in the complex societies we create, must also fool each other. After all, it simply wouldn't do for everyone around you to be aware of every angry, lusty, jealous, or selfish feeling you have. And, Nesse says, what better way to fool others than to fool ourselves first? So we keep our true motivations hidden in our unconscious, in a place even we can't recognize. We deny our real motivations, until they are revealed by a conflict.

So the first step, recognition of your problem, is not such a simple thing. Like the silent earth building up pressure before an earthquake, fault lines may be developing within you or your relationship outside of your awareness.

The easiest way to become sensitive to the emergence of new problems is simply to notice change. It's particularly difficult to be sensitive to the impact of change on your relationship when the change in your life is positive for you but negative for your other. You'll naturally want to deny the disparity, while your other may be quietly resentful or jealous. A relocation, for instance, may be positive for you but stressful for your other. Your promotion may be wonderful for you but intimidating to your other. A new friendship you have may be fun for you but diminish your availability to your other.

And, of course, vice versa: your other may welcome a particular change that may be painful for you. Some examples:

Sam was delighted when the last of his stepchildren left home for college. His wife was depressed about it.

Marie was thrilled to get a new job that meant more money, but it made Lewis feel even more like a loser in his job.

Denise was delighted with her assertiveness when she refused to go on business trips with Mac, while Mac felt increasingly remote from her.

An easy way to become more sensitive to the emergence of problems is to be aware of the impact of change. Watch what happens to your relationship when there is:

- Addition of a new family member

- Loss of a family member

- A health problem

- Promotion or demotion at work

- Adoption of a new hobby

- An active new friendship

- Change in religion

- Emergence of psychiatric problems

- Geographic relocation

- Start of an educational or training program

Any of these changes can trigger a change in relationship dynamics. Be sensitive to their impact.

If you're not in a relationship currently, the above changes can have an enormous impact on you as well. Without the buffering impact of a relationship, you are actually freer to react and adapt to change and to problems. That can be positive or negative, depending on how you evolve. The point is to be aware of the impact that change has on you, regardless of your relationship status. Change always creates problems, and problems stimulate evolution of some sort.

Defining Your Problem

Once you recognize that there is a problem, your next step is to define it in such a way that you can take positive action. Easier said than done! Each of us sees the world through a lens of our own that colors and distorts our perceptions of our selves and each other.

An example: Anna, Beth, Carol, Dina, and Ellen all ended relationships with their boyfriend in their late twenties and entered a period of singleness.

- Anna said her problem was due to her inadequacies as a woman. She had previously had an eating disorder and believed she had been dumped because she had gained some weight. She developed a major depression with storms of anxiety that left her incapacitated, further enacting the role of the helpless, defeated woman.

- Beth blamed her breakup on the untrustworthiness of her boyfriend in particular and men in general. She felt bitter and cynical and had great difficulty projecting enough pleasantness to be attractive to potential new boyfriends.

- Carol defined her problem as a fundamental mismatch with her boyfriend and felt some relief mingled with sadness and anger. She decided to go into therapy to understand why she had made several poor choices of men and to learn how she could do better next time. She eventually married.

- Dina, though quite angry at her boyfriend, took the maxim "Living well is the best revenge" to heart. She defined her problem as needing to get back to an enjoyable lifestyle and went on several extravagant vacations, which resulted in new financial problems.

- Ellen decided that she had had enough of boyfriends and that she just wasn't cut out for another relationship in the near future. She decided to go to graduate school and eventually settled into a new profession.

Any problem can be defined in a variety of ways.

How you define your problem determines how you will evolve.

Each of these five women had a particular, characteristic way of defining problems in her life. Those definitions led to specific, repetitive solutions. Anna was always self-doubting, depressed, and masochistic. Beth tended to blame others and refused to examine her own behavior. Carol always tried to look at events from a variety of perspectives and usually learned and grew from her life experiences. Dina generally had a hedonistic, somewhat manic way of warding off painful experiences. Ellen had lifelong problems with intimacy and used productivity to keep from getting too close to others.

All individuals develop characteristic ways of defining and reacting to their problems. Those reactions then create dynamics with others that reinforce those perceptions and patterns. Anna's masochism, for instance, often made others feel frustrated with her. When they finally expressed their exasperation, it reinforced her low self-esteem. Beth's cynicism was off-putting to others. When her friends or lovers withdrew from her, it only made her more distrustful.

So if you can identify the repetitive ways you deal with interpersonal problems, you can begin to respond in a more flexible, reality-based way. Listen to your words as you talk about your problems. You may hear yourself using phrases like "Men are just so . . ." or "Women always want . . ." or "Guys these days just seem to . . ." And those words can give you insight into the ways you distort your perception of problems in your life.

Anna, Beth, Carol, Dina, and Ellen were all partially correct in their respective views of their breakups, and they could actually have learned a lot from each other had they been able to entertain a complex understanding of their problem: all breakups are partially attributable to you, and partially to your other. All are partly due to a bad "match." Self-exploration is always helpful, as is getting out and having fun and investing more deeply in work or education. Yet each of them wanted to boil down complexity to a single issue. Unfortunately, that limited their capacity to evolve to just a single direction.

As you work on expanding your ability to evolve in positive directions, the best place to start is to redefine the significant problems in your life. But given that you could redefine your problems in any number of ways, how do you decide which way is best for you?

Always define your problems in ways that allow you to solve them.

Begin with the assumption that there is something you can do to improve, if not solve, the issue you're struggling with. Blaming the problem on someone else and playing the role of the victim gets you nowhere.

Gloria: The Disappointed Wife

Gloria had entered her marriage with high hopes. She and Laurence had a wildly romantic courtship, and she had been convinced that she had found the great love of her life. During that period, they had both been on their best behavior, and the sweet madness of true love allowed them to ignore some glaring faults in each other. Over the years, however, the relationship had morphed into an emotional standoff. Laurence was perpetually withdrawn and unwilling to talk with Gloria about the stresses he had at work. Gloria was chronically irritated by the double roles of homemaker and wage earner and was frustrated by Laurence's aloofness. She felt the lack of emotional support for herself and desperately yearned for companionship. They had two children and had overextended themselves with a large mortgage. Gloria often felt there was simply no way out.

Here are several ways Gloria could define her problems, each of which would lead to a different solution and different evolutionary path:

1. "Laurence is a jerk and he'll never change. He spends so much time in his cave that no wonder he has bats in his belfry. When the children are older, I'm going to blow this marriage."

2. "Okay, I admit I can be a real bitch. Maybe if I could do something about my temper, Laurence would want to spend more time with me."

3. "I'm just too dependent on Laurence. Maybe I should go out with some of the girls after work sometimes and make some new friends."

4. "Laurence and I just can't talk to each other anymore. Maybe somehow we could learn to communicate better."

The first definition was the only one that left Gloria unable to proactively work on her problem. Defining her problem as unsolvable could only make her feel sullen, hostile, and victimized. The other three solutions all allowed Gloria to actually do something about her problem in positive ways. The second definition would stimulate her to develop her ability to deal healthily with anger; the third would cause her to evolve her social skills; and the fourth would stimulate her to develop her ability to communicate. Any or all of those three definitions would be healthier than the first—even if it was also true that Laurence by nature had an aloof personality.

Define your problems in a way that stimulates you to evolve in the directions you desire to go.

If you were Gloria, which way of viewing your problem might best foster your personal growth?

The answer would reflect an issue that has repeatedly caused you problems. Perhaps you've always been shy and have never learned to develop close friends. By defining your problem as needing to draw social support outside your marriage, you could begin to develop new skills in making friends.

Perhaps other people in your life—your sibs, your kids, or your boss—have also remarked on your crabbiness. Learning more effective ways of dealing with conflicts might be the most important way you could grow.

Maybe it's not just Laurence who communicates poorly. Maybe that's been a problem for you, too, and learning to listen and express yourself better would be a great goal for marital therapy.

A rule of thumb: If a given situation is the first time you've ever had to deal with a particular dynamic, it's probably not your "fault." However, if you keep bumping against the same issues, if several people in your life have seemingly created the same problem for you, you need to look within.

Problems are messages.

Evolving to Solve Your Problem

Once you've recognized and defined your problem, there is of course the pesky little issue of how you go about solving your problem and evolving in the process. One overriding suggestion will make the process quicker, more interesting, and more likely to be successful:

Don't try to do it all by yourself. No matter how well-intentioned you are, it's hard to make major changes in yourself without talking to someone about it. Otherwise, when the problem of the moment has passed, you'll forget about your resolution to change—until the problem comes back again.

Talk with your other

The best person to talk to is the one you're having a problem with. Find a quiet, uninterrupted time to talk—when you're on a long car trip or after the kids are in bed. Open the conversation in a nonthreatening way, commenting on the difficulty that's occurring and how you'd like to work on your contribution to the situation. Ask your other for his or her suggestions and perceptions.

If your other is at all psychologically minded and interested in improving the relationship, he may also examine his own contribution to the problem. Don't be derailed, however, he is unable to accept ownership of his issues. Remember, you have only just taken responsibility for your own behavior, so it shouldn't be so surprising if he is lagging behind you. Remember that your goal is not to change your other but to consciously guide your own evolution. Perhaps your other will be inspired by your example; perhaps not.

So, if Gloria decided to talk, really talk, with Laurence about their communication problem, the conversation might go something like this:

GLORIA: Laurence, we don't talk so much anymore.

LAURENCE: *(grunt)*

GLORIA: Do you ever miss it?

LAURENCE: I dunno. Not really, I guess.

GLORIA: Well, I do. I wonder what I could do to make it easier for us to talk.

LAURENCE: I dunno. I guess I'd have to think about that.

GLORIA: Let me give you an example. Last week I suggested we go to my mother's house on Sunday. You didn't really say anything one way or the other, but when we got there, I could tell you really didn't want to be there. Why couldn't you have said that when I first brought it up? Is there anything I could have done to make it easier for you to speak up?

LAURENCE: C'mon, Gloria. You know that if I had said I didn't want to go, you'd have gotten all upset. I just figured it was easier to go along with what you wanted.

GLORIA: So maybe if I made it easier to say what you really felt, maybe if I didn't get bent out of shape, you'd feel more comfortable telling me.

LAURENCE: I dunno. Maybe.

Obviously, this single conversation did not open up a mother lode of meaningful conversation, and Laurence displayed his typical preference for terse responses to Gloria. But Gloria knew that Laurence had it in him to be more interactive, for she saw him open up more with their friends. Rather than becoming sullen, she committed herself to listening carefully to the few clues Laurence was willing to share and paid attention to his observation that her responses often made him shut down.

Talk with a friend
You may not be in a love relationship currently, or you may have an issue you can't discuss with your mate. It's important to find someone you can trust to talk with. Ask for honest feedback. Solicit ideas about new behaviors you could work on. Ask how this person has solved a similar problem.

Whether you're talking to your mate or to a platonic friend, it's scary to reveal your humility and vulnerability. You may believe that as long as you don't talk about your problem, no one will notice. You're wrong. You're the last to know.

A few years ago, I participated in a leadership program for women doctors. As part of our training, we divided up into groups and over a year had conference calls in which we openly discussed our professional issues and asked for feedback from others. It was humbling to be open about our shortcomings, but helpful.

One woman in my group, Lynda, was remarkably active about soliciting advice and even criticism from others. I told her I admired her ability to hear critical feedback about herself and to use it constructively.

"I really appreciate criticism," she said. "I don't learn anything from the compliments. But when someone criticizes you, they're usually saying something they've put some thought into. It helps me to grow so much more than all the positive comments."

Of course when your friend criticizes you or offers a specific suggestion, you owe it to yourself to examine whether you agree. Friends sometimes offer bad advice. Further, your friend's advice will be influenced by how you have described your problem; don't use the conversation just to get permission for what you wanted to do anyway. But that's why it's important to have several friends whose advice you generally trust. If you keep hearing the same messages over and over, pay attention. And if you find yourself rejecting everyone's advice, just make sure you understand why.

So, taking this step, Gloria would talk to one or more friends about why they thought Laurence and she couldn't talk. If she talked to three friends, she might hear:

> **FRIEND 1:** Gloria, men are just like that. Bill doesn't talk to me, either.

FRIEND 2: Gloria, how do you expect him to talk when you talk all the time?

FRIEND 3: Gloria, if you ask him to talk, remember that you have to actually listen. You have to accept what he says and make him feel something good came out of the conversation.

Gloria was wise enough not to be distracted from her goal by Friend 1. She knew that Friend 2 was joking, but in jokes there is always a kernel of truth: she did talk too much, and she began to wonder if that didn't make Laurence shut down. And the words of Friend 3 were truly useful. She realized that Laurence would talk if she could listen in a supportive, encouraging way.

Search for the problem beneath the problem
Remember that your personality functions as it does for good reasons—at least, reasons that made great sense at one time in your life. As you identify a way in which you'd like to change, spend some time wondering why you developed as you did to begin with. What purpose did your behavior originally serve? What were you afraid might happen if you acted otherwise? What do you fear might happen if you change?

As Gloria thought more deeply, she became aware that she talked a lot and listened poorly for a good reason: everyone in her family was like that. Well, not everyone. Her mother had not been a talker at all. Her mother had been depressed and rarely spoke, and her few utterances were predictably critical or negative. Gloria and her siblings had learned to chatter away to keep their mother quiet. They kept all conversation superficial so as not to give their mother the chance to be hurtful.

So it was understandable that Gloria relived that experience with Laurence. The more she talked, the less chance there was for him to say something hurtful. If he did challenge her, she quickly became defensive.

Gloria needed not only to be able to really listen. She had to become convinced that it was safe to listen, safe to give up control of airtime. She made a resolution to listen in an open, nondefensive way.

Resolve to evolve in all your relationships

When I first started in radio, a voice coach told me that I had to pitch my voice lower, to get rid of a breathy, little-girl quality. I quickly realized that I had to make it a habit to pitch lower all the time, not just when broadcasting. I couldn't just turn my voice off and on, because when I was broadcasting live, I needed to focus my attention on what I was saying, not on how my voice sounded.

Likewise, if you wish to truly evolve, practice your desired behavior in all your relationships, all the time. Don't just turn it off and on for your other, for your change will be superficial and transient. Practice at home, at work, at the grocery store, and with your mother.

Gloria's goal was to communicate better with Laurence, but in truth she needed to communicate better with everyone. Her anxiety-driven need to control conversations was not limited to Laurence but had become a mode of interacting. As her honest friend commented, it was often hard to get a word in edgewise with Gloria, and that had limited her ability to engage deeply even with her closest friend. She resolved to listen more in all her relationships, all the time.

Be patient

Real change does not occur quickly. You can begin to change your behavior today, but for that change to become automatic and reflex-

ive will take months, if not longer. Remember as well that just because you've changed doesn't mean that everyone around you will
instantly change. You're not evolving for the sake of manipulating
others' behavior, but for the sake of your own emotional growth.

You don't have to change 180 degrees to make a difference in
your life. Gloria and Laurence improved somewhat in their communication—say, 20 or 30 percent. But that was enough to make a
big difference in their relationship. Laurence learned to speak up
about what he did and did not want to do. Gloria learned to be
more aware of his feelings and sensitive to his wishes. As he became less resentful of her, he was able to be more giving and affectionate—a wonderful payoff for Gloria.

Revolution

If evolution were the only pathway to human growth, you'd be
stuck reacting to whatever your environment served up to you.
What distinguishes humans from other animals is that we possess
the intelligence and free will to rise out of our environment when
we need or want to.

Revolution begins by realizing that something in your environment constricts your ability to get the life you want. You've tried
to adapt or evolve to fit your surroundings, but all the evolution
you can muster will not allow you to achieve your goals. You finally decide that rather than continue to try to change yourself,
you must change something in your environment, often a particular relationship. Once you've made that change, evolving begins
all over again, hopefully in a more positive and healthy direction.

Examples of revolution:

- Breaking off a friendship or love affair
- Divorce

- Seeking a new relationship

- Changing your career

- Quitting your job

- Committing yourself to a new creative pursuit

- Joining a different religious group

While evolution is often an uncomfortable process, revolution can be downright threatening. Evolution allows you to stay within your safety zone, maintaining the secure relationships or environment that are familiar and predictable. Revolution demands taking a risk. You snip the strings of your familiar safety net before another one has been woven beneath you. Yet because it's so scary it's exciting.

There are people who compulsively and impulsively stage revolutions. They jump from job to job, romance to romance, interest to interest, or religion to religion. If you are a compulsive revolutionary, challenge yourself with the question *Why?* It may be that you don't have the discipline to tolerate the frustration of evolution. It may be that you deal with the anxiety of commitment by impulsive escapes. Evolution, after all, is a lot of work, and you may be using repeated revolutions to avoid the discomfort of real growth. Remember that to make progress toward the life you want, any healthy revolution is again followed by evolution; you may be avoiding the challenges of emotional development by bolting every time life gets frustrating.

But there are also people who are so terrified of taking risks that they suffer endlessly rather than revolt. They submerge their true desires and submit to the demands of others. The comfort of security and predictability is an opiate that sedates free will so much that they fall into a coma. They, too, will never get the life they want.

Signs That You've Overevolved

Your own evolution has allowed you to adapt to changes in your environment. It may be, though, that you have adapted so much that you have sacrificed a vital element of your core self. Yes, you fit in. Yes, you make life comfortable for everyone around you. But insidiously, invisibly, your evolution has left you feeling "not you" anymore. You have evolved in a direction that will not permit you to get the life you want.

Some of the markers of overevolution are:

- Losing sight of your original goals

- Betraying a spiritual value that is important to you

- Feeling trapped by your circumstances

- Never feeling happy, excited, or optimistic

- Sacrificing activities or relationships that once brought great pleasure

- A sense of flatness or resignation

Some deaths occur by ice, and some by fire. When you've overevolved you may die by microinches, gradually freezing into withdrawn paralysis. This may occur so quietly that you hardly recognize the chill until that part of you has been lost to frostbite. Or perhaps your death is occurring in a more dramatic way, with blazing anger and scorching arguments. It doesn't matter, really. Death is death, and if you feel yourself dying, it is time for a revolution.

Learning to Think for Yourself

Staging a revolution begins with thinking for yourself. That's not easy: throughout your life you have been taught to do the opposite. Your parents taught you to adopt their values and culture; you were a "good boy" or "good girl" if you did as you were told. In school, you had to learn to behave in class, and you mastered information that other people set before you; your duty was to learn what you were taught. You may belong to a religion that offers you a clear doctrine of what to believe; you are "good" if you adopt that doctrine on faith, not reason or logic. At work you are a "good worker" if you're a team player, if you subscribe to the values and goals of your company. Over and over again, you have been taught: goodness = not thinking for yourself.

Further, the necessity of social adaptation has taught you to challenge your own thinking and restrain yourself from expressing your needs and the impulses of the moment. Civilization, communities, and families, after all, are good things. They simply couldn't survive if individuals refused to play by rules.

There may, however, come a time in your life when the rules that have been established to support the social order have been hijacked in order to squelch your needs, destroy your dreams, and limit your rights.

You may be in a marriage in which your vows bind you to a mate who defeats your attempts to give and receive real love; yet the dictates of religion and society forbid you to leave. You may be in a job in which your employer uses legal contracts to take advantage of you or exploits your sense of responsibility for his or her own goals. Rules, norms, traditions, and legalities that stabilize society may squelch your chances to find the love you want.

The Case of Millie Benson

Millie Benson was a prolific writer. You may well have read several of her books without realizing it. She wrote under the pseudonym of Carolyn Keene and authored twenty-three of the original thirty Nancy Drew mysteries. Her financial reward for the best-selling series? One hundred and twenty-five dollars per book. She had signed a secrecy contract and never collected a dime of royalties from the books, movies, and board games that resulted from her creativity. Yes, she had "played by the rules," but the rules were extraordinarily unfair and exploitive of her. A newspaper article about Benson noted that she was not bitter and quoted her as saying, "I make no profit from anything in connection with [Nancy Drew] and I didn't make anything when I wrote. It was my contribution to the children of America." (John Seewer, Associated Press, *Bangor Daily News*, January 5–6, 2002.)

Benson's case represents only an extreme form of a more subtle exploitation that occurs throughout life. At times people's very "goodness" becomes the means by which they block themselves from getting the life they truly want. If you have a bit of Millie Benson in you, consider another form of the Golden Rule: Ask others to treat you as you would treat them.

Less dramatically, you may find yourself in a situation in which you have agreed to particular expectations that are just not working out well. Perhaps you're the adult child of an ill parent and your siblings have elected you to be the responsible one. They're able to move on with their lives and are only too happy to allow you to feel guilty if you even think about moving forward with your life. Maybe you have a spouse to whom you're unhappily married, but because he or she has a mental illness you don't feel you can leave.

Or maybe you committed yourself to a love relationship or a

friendship that simply isn't right for you. It's easy to justify leaving if your other is a bad person. But what if it's not so clear-cut? What if it's just that you're chronically bored or irritated or uncomfortable around that person? What if your relationship prevents you from developing in directions that allow you to reach your fullest potential?

Black-and-white situations are the easiest to decide. But there are always shades-of-gray situations that are not obvious, in which claims of responsibility or commitment must be weighed against the preciousness of your one and only life.

No one can resolve the shades-of-gray issues but you. To do so requires thinking for yourself. Learning to think for yourself is unnerving, exciting, challenging, and awesome, for you take responsibility for getting the life you want. It means you own your own life. All by yourself.

What Do You Want?

The hallmark of being able to think for yourself is the ability to answer a simple question: *What do you want?*

It's deeply ironic that such a simple question is so difficult to answer for many people, maybe for you. After all, you came into the world as an infant with clear, simple ideas of what you wanted, and you emitted ear-piercing screams to advise your caretakers of your wishes. By two you learned to say "Gimme!" and you may have thrown blue-in-the-face tantrums if you didn't get it. By grade school, though, you learned to suppress your impulses. As a teenager, fitting in with your friends became so important that you forgot to think about what you really wanted. As an adult the process is more or less complete, and you've learned to subordinate the question *What do I want?* to a host of competing demands.

Many of those demands are external. Your wishes compete with those of your spouse, children, friends, and workmates. Your wishes for "right now" may collide head-on with your needs to prepare for the future. The impulses you struggle with—to eat with abandon, drink too much, have secret sex with someone other than your spouse, or take things that you covet from other people—might land you in the hospital, the rehab clinic, or jail. That you can't always get what you want is indeed based on reality.

But there are internal prohibitions as well.

Perhaps you are held back from knowing what you really want by the messages you received from your parents about what they wanted for you. Perhaps you are showing your loyalty to them by living out their lives, not yours. Maybe you feel that you're not worthy to get the life you want, or that to reach toward your desires is selfish. You may worry about making others jealous, or being rejected for your success or happiness.

To get in touch with what your deepest wishes are, take a few moments right now and make a wish list. Write down anything that comes to mind, no matter how fantastic, wicked, or out of reach those wishes are.

1. Imagine yourself a year after your death, looking back on the life you've lived. What do you wish you'd done differently?

2. Think of several of the people in life you most admire. What is it about their lives that you would most like to model yourself after?

3. What would you do for a day, a month, or a year if you had complete freedom and no one was watching?

4. What would you do with yourself if earning money were not a need?

5. How would you live your life if you had no responsibilities and had made no promises to others?

I am not advising that you take all of the secret wants you identified on your wish list, quit your job, leave your family, and blow town. Yet your wish list may reveal parts of yourself that you could honor and express, either by evolving toward new goals or by having a revolution when the time is right. Pay attention to the recurrent themes that dominate your wish list. Isn't there some way, any way, that you could come closer to reaching them? If your life depended on realizing your dreams, what would you do?

There are doubtless elements on your wish list that are unethical or unrealistic to act out directly. But couldn't some of those elements be transformed into realistic wishes that you could achieve? Maybe your list includes becoming a glamorous actress—not too realistic for most of us. But you could work on improving your figure or take an acting or modeling class. Maybe your list includes having sex with multiple partners at will. Also not a great idea. But you could work on becoming more romantic and sensual with the partner you have. These would be evolutionary changes—gradual and adaptive to your current environment.

But then something on your list will be really important to take at face value. Maybe that "something" reflects years of feeling frustrated and impotent about an aspect of your life.

Don't be so quick to write it off as unrealistic. It may be time for a revolution.

Closing the Door on Part of Your Life: Good-Byes

All revolution involves cutting ties with something in your life that's not working. Usually that means saying good-bye or creating some distance between you and someone you've been close to. Good-byes are always painful, and the person you are leaving may be hurt or angry. You may be moving on to something more positive in your life, but for the one left behind it's simply a loss.

Often that person may respond by trying to make you feel guilty about your actions. Guilt is a curious emotion. We may use guilt to reassure ourselves that we really are good people, as if to say, "Perhaps I didn't do the right thing, but look how guilty I feel about it." Theoretically and ideally, one should never have to feel guilt, which is an emotion that signals you're doing something against your moral standards. If you really are doing something immoral and unethical, don't. If what you are planning to do is not immoral or unethical, don't hammer yourself with guilt. You may feel concern, compassion, or responsibility toward the one you are leaving, but you don't have to put on a hair shirt.

There are farewells and then there are farewells. As painful as it is to say good-bye, there are things you can do in a spirit of graciousness that will make your ending easier:

- Give the person (or people) plenty of notice before you depart.

- Take ownership for the reasons behind your decision. Don't blame it on someone else.

- Express your feelings of appreciation for the good parts of your relationship.

- Don't bad-mouth the person or people you're leaving once you've left.

- Don't betray confidences you received in your relationship.

- Hold on to the good memories from the relationship.

Choosing a New Direction

Most often when you stage a revolution, you have some idea of what your next direction will be. Perhaps you are ending a relationship because you have identified someone else you want to be with. Perhaps you're leaving a career with another job in mind. Often, in fact, people will overstay their visit in one situation until they have a clear idea of something "out there" that would be more satisfying.

At times, though, you may leave without knowing what lies ahead. You may be in a difficult relationship and have decided that you'd rather be alone than be unhappy. Perhaps you've left a career and have the luxury of being able to take some time off before beginning something new. Taking a time-out between relationships can be useful to sort out your thoughts.

If you're in an unsatisfactory relationship, it's tempting to stay in the relationship "until something better comes along." Many a relationship limps along far too long for that reason, because as long as your time and energy are tied up, you won't have the motivation to really look. Remember that you can't say yes to what you do want unless you can say no to what you don't want.

Peter: In Quest of a New Love

Peter, thirty-eight, had been married for fourteen years when he began to feel that his dissatisfaction was reaching the breaking point. His wife, Cindy, was a mercurial, hot-tempered woman whose love of good Scotch further added to her unpredictability. It was hard, in fact, for Peter's friends to understand just why he had stayed with Cindy so long. The simple truth was that Peter was afraid to be alone.

So Peter resolved to stay in his marriage until "someone better" came along. Sure enough, he met Gwen, whose great attraction was that she was nothing like Cindy. Where Cindy was volatile, Gwen was even-tempered. Where Cindy was a party animal, Gwen liked to stay at home. Peter and Gwen hooked up, fell in love, and Peter gave Cindy the heave-ho. Cindy, of course, bitterly denounced Peter for his infidelity, ignoring her contribution to the demise of the marriage.

Why did Peter choose Gwen? Largely because she wasn't at all like Cindy. The problem, though, was that not only did she lack Cindy's weaknesses, but she lacked her strengths as well. Peter had, after all, had some good reasons for choosing Cindy. She was bright, funny, and adventuresome. Gwen, though a gentle, even-tempered person, was wholly dependent on Peter for friends and dealt with her anger in passive-aggressive ways. She had few intellectual or social interests, and Peter soon found himself bored and restless.

Often you feel a sense of emotional triumph when you finally decide to revolt. The excitement of that moment allows you to escape any memories of the past. But because someone is different from your last other doesn't guarantee that you'll be happier.

A quiet time between relationships allows you to reflect on the good parts of your last love, and don't be afraid to look for them in your next relationship. You can avoid the bad parts without throwing away all traits you associate with your last lover.

Stagnation

Stagnation occurs when you are neither evolving nor revolting. Think of a stagnant pond of water, green, murky, and stale. It cannot be said that nothing is happening in that pond—in fact, quite a bit is happening, for the pond is becoming less and less healthy for anything except algae.

Stagnation is a choice and a willful process.

You may feel as if stagnation is a default position, a state you enter when better choices seem unavailable. In fact, you always have better choices than stagnation. There is always something you can do to grow and improve you life.

There is no such thing as a simple "holding pattern" due to the nature of the human brain. The nerve cells in your brain are living, always responding to your environment. In some ways, they are similar to your muscle cells. If you use your muscles, they will remain firm and active. If you don't use a muscle, it will atrophy and shrink before your eyes. Likewise, if you use your brain cells, they grow and strengthen their connections to other brain cells. If you stop using those brain cells, those connections are progressively lost.

Further, if your behavior becomes rote—if you're merely going through the motions of love or work, for instance—you're strengthening particular habits. You're training and retraining your brain not to respond to novelty, not to actively listen, see, think, feel, not to be creative. The habit patterns of not responding to others become automatic.

Certainly, the people around you, whether at home or at work, will not experience your stagnation as a simple lack of growth. They will experience you as frustrating, irritating, and passive aggressive. They will feel cheated of your full participation, and they'll resent you for it. They will perceive that consciously or unconsciously you are withholding yourself from them, as active and willful a choice as participating with them.

Stagnation as a Single Person

Stagnation is an equal-opportunity experience, possible whether you're single or married. Stagnation is often not a problem in the first years of singlehood, whether that occurs in your twenties or after the breakup of a relationship or marriage. But as time goes on and months turned into years or even decades, it becomes easier and easier to withdraw from opportunities and challenges. Solitude feels comfortable and secure, if somewhat flat and boring. You begin to develop patterns of behavior that allow you to settle into your comfort zone, safe within your home or in the company of an old friend or two. Some signs that you have begun to stagnate include:

- You've not made a new friend in over a year
- You've not taken a vacation in over a year
- You turn down invitations to social functions where you might meet someone
- You avoid taking business trips
- You develop set routines for Friday and Saturday nights
- Your mother has become your best friend
- You're in your pajamas by eight at night
- You turn down blind dates
- You choose to live in a geographically or socially isolated place
- You dress sloppily in situations where you might meet someone new
- You turn down spontaneous invitations from close friends

- You prefer long-distance conversations to going out

- You've gone up two sizes in the past five years

- You drink more than two drinks a day if you're a woman, or more than three drinks a day if you're a man

- Your home is too messy to invite people over

- You'd rather sleep with a pet than a human

Guard against stagnation. Make a friend, go on vacation, change your look, put away the booze, and clean your house. Most importantly, engage.

Stagnation in Marriage

Your primary love relationship—marriage, for most people—offers you abundant opportunities to evolve your capacity to love. It's impossible to hide your most significant interpersonal issues in a marriage. Time is a powerful spotlight that reveals the true colors of your heart, mind, and character. Yet it's also possible to use marriage to hide from problems.

As a love relationship develops over the months and years, you and your mate increasingly reveal your true selves to each other. You may realize that the person you fell in love with is not the person you are now married to, and your spouse realizes the same. Some marriages continue to grow in love and loyalty nonetheless. Marriages in evolution change in response to the inevitable problems that accumulate in a relationship.

There is, of course a second choice—revolution. Divorce is the ultimate form of revolution. Much like the initial decision to marry, divorce may be a wise decision, a foolish impulse, a way of avoiding other problems, or the beginning of a path to new growth.

But that third choice, stagnation, is unfortunately all too common. You're neither happily married nor are you divorced and getting on with a new life. You've decided to stay in your marriage for whatever reason—the kids, money, or perhaps your fear of the unknown. But you've also decided to withdraw from your spouse. You may or may not bicker or argue from time to time. But you hold secret grudges within you, like scar tissue around your heart that keeps you from truly connecting with your spouse.

When you've made that third choice, you remain physically in the marriage but psychologically live in your inner world. Often this takes the form of fantasizing about romantic adventures with other people. You may even put yourself on the lookout, waiting for an opportunity for such an adventure. You may actually have affairs, whether one-night stands or lengthier involvements. Perhaps you find yourself imagining what life would be like if your spouse were dead.

Some people who have made the third choice become pros at faking their way through their marriages. They may feel that addressing their problems is pointless, for their spouse seems incapable of change. Perhaps they feel so fundamentally mismatched that no amount of communication or effort will address the basic problem in the marriage. So they put up and shut up, going through the motions, often convincingly, of pleasing their spouse. When these marriages end, others may say, "My God, I always thought they were so happy."

If you are currently making the third choice in your marriage, my advice is simple: don't. You're wasting your life as well as your spouse's, and it's unfair to both of you. It's like putting great time and energy into building the frame and walls of a house that has a weak foundation, and in time your marriage may come tumbling down like a house of cards.

You're undoubtedly making the third choice because there are good reasons for not getting out of your marriage. Use those good reasons to inspire you to really get back into your marriage—the first choice. Don't make the too common mistake of waiting until one of you wants out, for by then it's too late. Do everything you can to make your marriage as good as it can possibly be—and only then make your decision.

If you've really committed yourself to the first choice for an extended period and you cannot, really cannot, heal your marriage, the time may come when you should consider the second choice—divorce. Having been through a divorce, I can attest that it is a terribly painful experience, sometimes as painful as widowhood. Not only do you grieve the loss of that person in your life, but you have the additional problems of bitterness, betrayal, and the miserable legal process of salvaging your financial life. But there is new life on the other side of a divorce, and it's fairly rare to hear people say they regret the decision.

Increasing Your Capacity to Change

The ability to change, whether through evolution or revolution, is essential to finding and maintaining the love you want so much. But the larger issue is, is it possible to actually increase your capacity to change? Is it possible to reach deep within yourself and decrease your resistance to change and growth?

Of course you can increase your ability to change—but you do that not by reaching within yourself but by reaching outside yourself. The human mind is somewhat like a computer. Without the input of new programs or data, the computer is limited in its ability to perform a range of tasks. On the other hand, a powerful computer has a seemingly limitless ability to perform new tasks so long as its operator gives it new information.

The easiest way to increase your capacity to change is to stimulate your mind with new ideas, new experiences, and new relationships. Combine that stimulation with a commitment to be open to change and a drive to find love, and your have a winning recipe. You can think of increasing your capacity to change as an evolution in itself.

Some of the ways to stimulate your mind include:

Read more. If you bought this book in the self-help section of your local bookstore, you know that many wonderful books are available to educate you about personal growth and development. But don't limit your reading to only the self-help section. Fiction, history, and biographies can offer startling insights. They provide you with models of remarkable people to inspire you on your personal journey.

Reach outside your social circle. Observe that with your closest friends, wonderful though they may be, you tend to repeat the same ideas and reinforce the same values. Spending time with people very different from you will expose you to new ways of thinking.

Listen. As you walk through your daily life, listen to the words of people you meet. Absorb the stories they tell and the ideas they share. Sometimes the simplest of conversations may jar your thinking and send you in a new direction. Make notes about interesting conversations you've had, ideas you've had, and write them down in a journal.

Observe. Imagine that you were a writer or a journalist. What might you see as you walk through your daily life that stimulates new ideas? What behaviors do you observe in people you admire that you might learn from?

Step outside yourself. Examine your behavior. Consider the range of options you have at any time and how they might lead to different results. Identify people you admire, and imagine how they might respond to the same challenges and problems you have.

Challenge Your Big Assumptions

Psychologist Dr. Robert Kegan studies work-related behaviors and organizations and has written about a concept he calls "challenging your big assumptions." Big assumptions are the convictions that guide the choices you make. In the business world, for example, a big assumption might be "It's good to make a lot of money" or "You always have to look out for number one." That sort of assumption might be the basis of many decisions and go unchallenged until you consciously examine your behavior.

Challenging your big assumptions is important in your love life as well. Some big assumptions that you might wish to challenge to get the love you want include:

"If I compromise, I won't be respected."

"You can't really expect men to talk about their feelings."

"Women are unreliable."

"Little white lies don't make a difference."

"I should never relocate for the sake of a relationship."

"It's wrong to divorce."

"I couldn't possibly deal with a man's children from a former marriage."

"I could never marry a younger man."

An infinite number of big assumptions hold people back from getting the love they want. Sit down for moment and think about yours. What are your "sacred cows" that get in the way of finding love? Which is more important, your big assumption or a life of love?

And Finally, Ask Yourself, "Am I Happy?"

Modern culture has a marked ambivalence about happiness. On the one hand, there is a justifiable backlash against hedonism. We have become an instant-gratification society, and impulsively grabbing the closest sexual thrill, material item, or designer drug is a problem of contemporary society. The voices that express concern about compulsive happiness-seeking are wise.

On the other hand, deeper levels of happiness are often paid short shrift.

The fast pace and high demands of modern living make it all too easy to sprint from hour to hour and day to day. Core questions like "Am I at peace with my life?" "Do I genuinely love my lover?" "Is this marriage working for me?" are easily swept under the carpet.

But there's something in between hedonistic obsession with pleasure and denial of the importance of creating a core of happiness deep within you. If you're aware that the choices you've made can never allow you to find serenity, fulfillment, and, yes, occasional joy, pay attention. That recognition is essential for you to create the motivation to change.

One Last Story

It's appropriate to end with the story of a woman who successfully found love. In fact, it required committing herself to all five Essential behaviors to reach her goal of getting married.

We'll call her Patty. Patty was thirty-seven, had never married, and had a good job in a midsized Midwestern town. She had friends, a good salary, and a reasonably full life. It would have been a great life—for someone else. She wanted a husband and children.

She decided it was time for a revolution.

First, she believed that her chances of finding true love in her town were limited. It was a company town, and the vast majority of people who lived there were solid family types. She observed many lovely single young women in her company who never had a date, much less a relationship.

So she decided she had to relocate. She made several trips to larger cities, interviewed for a number of jobs, and chose a job that would bring her into contact with a lot of people. She knew no one in her new hometown. She was alone.

However, the goal to which she had committed herself was central in her mind, and so she purposefully outlined a program to meet people. She chose an apartment in a complex with a lot of single people. She joined a health club that had coed classes and activities. She joined a church with a large following of people her age and a singles group. She signed up for a dating service and also began to use a telephone dating service that allowed her to hear the voices of prospective candidates.

Patty lucked out fairly early and met a man whom she started dating. Within a few months, though, he told her that he found her overly possessive and broke off the relationship. She realized that he was correct in his perception and began to be worried that she might persistently sabotage herself. So she found a psychotherapist with whom she worked for almost a year.

She did, in fact meet a man through the dating service who really was right for her. They fell in love, married, and she now has her baby.

Does Patty's behavior sound extreme to you? It was—but it worked. Each thing she did increased her chances somewhat of finding someone to love. She couldn't predict ahead of time which was the magic ticket, so she committed herself to doing as many things as she could.

There is an element of magic—or luck or chance or fate—about meeting "the right one." That makes it easier for you to rationalize not doing the sort of things Patty did. It's always easy to say, "Well, I tried a dating service [once]." "Well, I never met anyone at the gym [during the three months I actually went]." "Well, blind dates just never worked out for me [two years ago]."

If you're really serious about finding love, make it your top priority. Break a rule or two. Learn to engage. Evaluate your choices, and for God's sake, don't let your anxiety mess it all up. Keep your emotional independence, and please do remember to evolve as your relationship does.

It's so important.

INDEX

ABOUT THE AUTHOR

DR. LINDA AUSTIN is host of the nationally broadcast public radio program, *What's On Your Mind?* Her previous book, *What's Holding You Back?: Eight Critical Choices for Women's Success*, was featured on the *Oprah Winfrey Show* and other national media. As Professor of Psychiatry at the Medical University of South Carolina, she lectures nationally on issues of women's development. Recently she was honored by the National Library of Medicine as an influential woman leader in American medicine. Dr. Austin is the mother of two grown children and lives in Bangor, Maine, with her husband. She teaches at Eastern Maine Medical Center and continues a busy psychiatric practice.